GRACE &
JUSTIFICATION

GRACE & JUSTIFICATION

*An Evangelical's Guide
to Catholic Beliefs*

STEPHEN WOOD

FAMILY LIFE CENTER
PUBLICATIONS
www.Dads.org

ISBN: 9780972757188
Library of Congress Control Number: 2017941996
Book production: Family Life Center Publications
Cover and layout design: 5sparrows.com
Manufactured in the United States of America

Acknowledgments

I would like to thank Drs. Christian Washburn and Kenneth Howell for their valuable advice. I also thank Lucy Allen, Connie Brushaber and several other friends for their assistance with and suggestions for the text. All remaining errors and omissions are mine.

Family Life Center Publications
2130 Wade Hampton Blvd.
Greenville, SC 29615

www.Dads.org

Table of Contents

CHAPTER ONE

My Introduction to Justification by God's Grace

S tanding on the sidewalk outside an expansive Southern California convention center, I was utterly confused as I tried to follow a heated theological argument between two friends. Sensing my perplexity, one friend turned toward me, and looked directly into my eyes, and said, "Steve, never forget the grace of God."

At the time, I was just beginning my formal theological studies. There would be scores of conflicting theological positions I'd be studying and evaluating in the years ahead. Little did I realize the enormity of the task facing a sincere Protestant seeking the fullness of truth and starting from scratch.

Although my friend who said, "Steve, never forget the grace of God" wasn't a famous theologian, pastor, or author, his words have guided my spiritual pilgrimage through countless classes, commentaries, conferences and confusing theological conflicts. "Never forget the grace of God" has been the North Star in my theological journey.

There are two things that are fundamental to the inner core of my being. First, I am acutely aware that I am a sinner entirely deserving eternal punishment in hell for my actions and attitudes toward God. I identify with St. Paul who said, "I am the foremost of sinners; but I received mercy" (1 Tim 1:15–16). The second fundamental in my life is that receiving mercy, forgiveness, and salvation is through the grace of Jesus Christ. Since the night I knelt by my bunk on the U.S.S. *Coronado* and asked Christ to forgive my sins, the grace of Jesus Christ has been the core of my life.

The main reason I never seriously considered becoming a Catholic for nearly two decades stemmed from the constantly reinforced claim that Catholicism denied the grace of God. If the Catholic Church denied God's grace, then I wanted no part of it. In addition, I believed it was my Christian charitable duty to lead Catholics away from their "grace-denying" church into a "Bible-believing" church.

If anyone claims that the Catholic Church denies that salvation is by the grace of God, he doesn't know what he's talking about. I know what I'm talking about when I talk about people who don't know what they are talking about because I was such a person.

It doesn't matter if the person has a doctorate in theology, a nation-wide religious broadcast, or if he pastors a mega-church. If he says the Catholic Church teaches that salvation is by our own efforts and not by the grace of God, you are listening to someone who is misinformed.

For starters, the Catholic Church formally condemned the belief that we can earn salvation by ourselves fifteen centuries ago at the Council of Carthage (A.D. 418). The heretic Pelagius was promoting a "do-it-yourself" type of salvation. Evidently,

Pelagius blamed the moral laxity he observed in Rome on the theology of grace. St. Jerome and St. Augustine vigorously opposed the heretical teachings of Pelagius and defended St. Paul's theology of grace. Pelagius was formally denounced as a heretic by the Catholic Church.[1]

Therefore, the belief that you can save yourself and do good works apart from divine grace has been formally rejected by the Catholic Church for a millennium and a half.

So if the Catholic Church doesn't believe in a "do-it-yourself type of salvation," what does it believe about grace and justification? Here is the answer straight from the *Catechism of the Catholic Church*. For any informed discussion on the Catholic beliefs on justification, paragraph 1996 is the most important section in the *Catechism*:

> **Our justification comes from the grace of God**. Grace is *favor*, the *free and undeserved help* that God gives us to respond to his call to become children of God, adoptive sons, partakers of the divine nature and of eternal life.[2]

The next time you hear someone claim that Protestants believe in justification by grace (undeserved mercy) and that Catholics believe in justification only by human works, please don't fall for the misrepresentation. The *Catechism of the Catholic Church* is the sure norm for Catholic beliefs, and it explicitly states, "Our justification comes from the grace of God."

Paragraph 1996 isn't an isolated catechism text. Paragraph 2003, focusing on the Holy Spirit's role in salvation, says, "Grace is first and foremost the gift of the Spirit who justifies and sanctifies us." Paragraph 1998 says, "This vocation to eternal life is *supernatural*. It depends entirely on God's gratuitous initiative."

3

It may be a surprise for some, as it was for me, to learn that *both* Protestants and Catholics believe in justification by grace. So what causes the big division over justification between Protestants and Catholics? The debate isn't over one side believing in justification by grace and the other side denying it. The big split is over different understandings of the work of grace in our justification.

For twenty years I taught and preached about the grace of God in salvation and the Protestant belief that justification was by faith *alone*. I was utterly convinced that I was correct in my understanding. Hadn't I intensely researched St. Paul's Epistles, including a careful study of the Greek text of his Epistles? Wasn't it right to lump Catholicism with the other false religions that fatally believe in a "do-it-yourself" method of salvation? Didn't Catholicism deny the grace of God, teaching that we earn our own salvation apart from God's grace? Wasn't Catholicism just like first-century legalistic Judaism, which St. Paul said was accursed?

I wasn't going to budge one inch toward a church that taught salvation by self-generated works (i.e., human effort apart from God's grace). Yet, after twenty years as an Evangelical Protestant,[3] something prompted me to question whether I really understood the Catholic beliefs on justification. Was I really rejecting Catholicism, or was I rejecting a caricature of Catholicism? I knew I had some investigating to do, but it was difficult finding straight answers.

I can say with the authority that comes from two decades of personal experience that the vast majority of Evangelical Protestants do not understand Catholic beliefs on justification. To make matters worse, most Catholics don't understand either the Protestant beliefs on justification, or their own. In fact, over a twenty-year period as an Evangelical Protestant, I *never* met a Catholic who could explain accurately the Catholic beliefs pertaining to justification. This greatly reinforced all my misconceptions.

My Purpose, My Hopes, and My Motivation

My purpose in writing this book is to provide clear and reliable answers to *both* Evangelical Protestants and Catholics on the questions surrounding grace and justification. I believe God allows us to go through certain struggles in order to become sensitive to the needs of others experiencing similar things (2 Cor 1:3–5). Therefore, I am writing a nontechnical book, especially for Evangelical pastors, elders, deacons, and serious laymen, that I wish I had had during my search for the fullness of the Church. I'll be presenting both the Protestant and the Catholic beliefs on grace and justification.[4] In addition, I'll explain why those from each perspective believe what they do.

My hope for Catholic readers is that you will understand your faith on this topic and be able to defend, explain, and contrast it to Protestant beliefs, using the Bible as common ground. Charity demands that Catholics equip themselves to share their faith with others. I'm not talking about bitter debates and theological wrangling, but respectful, knowledgeable, and charitable dialogue on this most critical issue dividing Protestants and Catholics.

My hope for Protestant readers is that the grand obstacle to even considering Catholicism might be removed. Yes, there are many other important questions to consider about Catholicism, but getting the questions about grace and justification answered is the first critical step.

I want my Protestant readers to know that I don't consider the Catholic faith to be the antithesis of Evangelicalism. In fact, I regard myself as an Evangelical Catholic. For me, becoming a Catholic has been to discover a depth of Christian fulfillment that was awakened by my rewarding experiences in Evangelicalism.

My motivation for writing this book isn't just to prove one side right and the other side wrong. There are plenty of both Protestant and Catholic books like that. I am writing because I am a very unworthy person who has been graced with a glance into the greatness of divine grace.

Evangelicals have a commendable motivation to share with others how to have a life-changing personal relationship with Christ. In like manner, I want Evangelicals considering Catholicism to know that becoming a Catholic intensifies their personal relationship with Christ—and his Father.

To truly understand justification, you'll want to learn more than some abstract doctrinal subjects. Therefore, don't just jump into an analysis of doctrine. Make your search to understand justification a facet of a greater search to know God himself.

Therefore begin and continue your journey with prayer to know God. Ask the Father for the Holy Spirit, the spirit of sonship. Seek the light of Christ that will enlighten your mind to God's Fatherhood. Knock and keep knocking on heaven's gates until the door to the Father's heart opens wide to you. Once opened, this door not only gives understanding to justification, it opens the door to the entire mystery of the Father's gracious plan of salvation.

For this reason I bow my knees before the Father ... that Christ may dwell in your hearts through faith; that you, being rooted and grounded in love, may have power to comprehend with all the saints what is the breadth and length and height and depth, and to know the love of Christ which surpasses knowledge, that you may be filled with all the fulness of God. (Eph 3:14, 17–19)

My wish for both Protestant and Catholic readers is that you obtain a deeper knowledge of and love for God the Father, his Son Jesus Christ, and the Holy Spirit.

Methodology for Discovering St. Paul's Teaching on Justification

I would like to suggest a methodology I learned from John Calvin to determine whether the Protestant or Catholic understanding of grace is the correct one. In the opening section of Calvin's *Institutes of the Christian Religion,* he asks the reader to compare carefully his teaching and the teaching of the Catholic Church with the writings of the Church Fathers.[5] He was convinced that his *Institutes* would win the day.

Well, I did exactly what John Calvin suggested and ended up leaving Calvinism for Catholicism. Calvin didn't realize that he had made a huge historical mistake by neglecting to compare his teaching with the seven epistles of St. Ignatius, one of the earliest of the Church Fathers, who heard apostolic teaching firsthand. It was a common scholarly error in Calvin's generation to lump together and disregard the seven genuine epistles of St. Ignatius along with the seven spurious epistles attributed to Ignatius. As an Evangelical Presbyterian, I was shocked to learn that the *Institutes of the Christian Religion* didn't make for harmonious reading with the seven genuine epistles of St. Ignatius.

Here's a modification of Calvin's methodology that will help you decide whether the Protestant or Catholic understanding of justification by grace is correct. This method involves carefully comparing the Protestant and Catholic beliefs on justification with St. Paul's teaching in his Epistle to the Romans. The correct belief will be that which (1) most closely adheres to *all* of St. Paul's teaching on justification by grace in Romans and (2) most gloriously exalts God's work of grace in our justification.

If you are an Evangelical reader, my methodology may surprise you. You may never have heard the claim that Catholicism exalts the grace of God to a greater degree than Protestantism does. It's my belief, after having spent twenty years as a Protestant and twenty-seven years as a Catholic, that the Catholic faith does a better job of exalting God's grace in justification.

I'm not asking my Evangelical readers to consider Catholicism correct if it has just a hidden-in-the-shadows perspective of grace and justification. I ask you to consider Catholicism only if you see that it gloriously exalts St. Paul's teaching on justification by grace and that it does so in a way as obvious as a volcano erupting. I realize that my claim may seem utterly preposterous to an Evangelical, but if you are willing to give authentic Catholic teaching a fair hearing, you may find yourself speechless and on your knees.

Are Catholics Complete Idiots?

If you are an Evangelical, ask yourself these questions: Why would Catholics do something so utterly stupid as to keep the Epistle to the Romans around if it was so threatening to their core beliefs on salvation? Why not just neglect it and eventually destroy the existing manuscripts? Why in the world would the Catholic Church carefully preserve this Epistle if it was so contrary to their unbroken teaching on justification?

Did it ever strike you as significant that this important Epistle was written by St. Paul to the church at Rome and that it has been in a treasured possession of the Catholic Church at Rome ever since? Do you think there's at least a slight chance that the church at Rome just might also have an accurate interpretation of the Epistle written to them two thousand years ago?

As an Evangelical, I studied Romans intensely for two decades. After reading what Protestant authors said in secondary resources, I thought that Catholics were so far off-base in their interpretation of Romans that I never bothered with a firsthand study of Catholic interpretations of the Epistle. I put the possibility of Catholic views on justification being true in the same category of the possibility that UFO abductions are really taking place in New Mexico. I didn't think science fiction abduction tales, nor what I supposed was theological nonsense, were worth my time.

I can testify that when I finally understood the authentic Catholic interpretation of Romans it was an eye-opening experience. In fact, once you give the Catholic interpretation of Romans a fair hearing, you'll see that it is entirely faithful to St. Paul's message. You'll find that the Catholic interpretation, rather than denying or distorting Romans, enriches Paul's priceless teaching on justification. You'll discover a deeper personal relationship with God as a result.

I know that many of my Evangelical readers think what I'm describing is not just improbable, but impossible. I know how you feel about Catholicism and Romans, but you truly owe it to yourself to see firsthand the Catholic view of Romans. After all, it was the Catholic Church headquartered at Rome that first received this Epistle from St. Paul.

You'll have to see for yourself if Catholicism lives up to my claim. In the meantime, I'd ask one thing of every reader: "Never, never, never forget the grace of God."

Chapter Two

How to Discover What Catholics Really Believe

Too few Protestants and Catholics accurately know what the official teaching of the Catholic Church really is on justification. Surprisingly, the confusion over justification extends to some Catholic leaders and authors.

Therefore, it is necessary to choose the best resources to discover authentic Catholic teaching. Choose the wrong ones, and you could end up more confused than when you began your study.

Catechism of the Catholic Church

The most up-to-date authoritative reference for any and all Catholic beliefs is the *Catechism of the Catholic Church.*

In the introduction to this catechism, Pope St. John Paul II wrote:

> The *Catechism of the Catholic Church* ... is a statement of the Church's faith and of catholic doctrine, attested to or illumined by Sacred Scripture, the Apostolic Tradition, and the Church's Magisterium. I declare it to be a sure norm for teaching the faith and thus a valid and legitimate instrument for ecclesial communion.[1]

Therefore, the single best place to go for reliable answers about Catholic beliefs on justification is the *Catechism*, especially paragraphs 1987 through 2029, entitled, "Grace and Justification." Read these pages carefully since they are essential for discovering the Catholic beliefs on justification. Yet before scrutinizing paragraphs 1987 through 2029, taking a simple preliminary step will reveal an overall understanding of the *Catechism of the Catholic Church* that is missed by many.

How to Read the *Catechism of the Catholic Church*

Mortimer Adler, one of the most brilliant authors of the twentieth century, wrote a valuable book entitled *How to Read a Book.* Adler changed the way many read books. It is easy to jump right in and read a book from cover to cover, but in the end one gains only a rudimentary understanding of the author's message.

In *How to Read a Book,* Adler teaches the discerning reader how an investment of just a few minutes before reading a book can reveal the author's purpose, theme, and structure. Following Adler's method unlocks the forest view of a book, whereas by the usual method the reader wanders from tree to tree without having a solid grasp of the author's overall message.

There is an often unnoticed book entitled "*Introduction to the Catechism of the Catholic Church*" that "Adlerizes" the entire *Catechism*. It should be required reading for anyone desiring not to get lost amidst the thousands of details in the 904 pages of the *Catechism*. This brief book was written by Joseph Cardinal Ratzinger, head of the commission appointed to prepare the *Catechism*, and by Christoph Schönborn, the editor for the *Catechism*'s commission. These two men reveal the purpose for the *Catechism*'s overall structure and arrangement.

There are four principal parts of the *Catechism* (Creed, Sacraments, Commandments, Prayer). The first two sections, describing who God is, what he has done on our behalf, and how he conveys those blessings to us through the sacraments, are intentionally placed first in order to give a "strong emphasis on the primacy of grace. God is first; grace is first. This is the true hierarchy of truth ... to the praise of his grace."[2]

Therefore, a person wanting to know what the Catholic Church truly believes about grace and justification, should not just study paragraphs 1987 through 2029, but observe the explicit intention that "the theme of grace runs through the whole *Catechism*."[3]

What about the *Catechism*'s stressing the importance of the Ten Commandments? Isn't that emphasis just the type of legalism that St. Paul condemns in Romans and Galatians? The answer is an emphatic "no."

Christoph Schönborn, the editor of the *Catechism*, says that when describing the Ten Commandments, "here too there must be no doubt about the primacy of grace."[4] He insists that "only when he recognizes the supernatural power that flows from ... being in Christ can the faithful disciple ... practice the Christian life in faithfulness to the Decalogue."[5] In Catholicism, keeping the Ten Commandments isn't a "do-it-yourself" moral effort, or a naked willpower exercise, but one that depends deeply upon grace.

The quickest and most accurate way to grasp what the Catholic Church really believes about grace and justification is first to read the book *Introduction to the "Catechism of the Catholic Church"* (less than a hundred pages), and then read paragraphs 1987 through 2029 (only ten pages) from the *Catechism* itself.

When you finish doing these simple steps you may find yourself wondering, "Why are so many still 'protesting' Catholicism?"

The Canons and Decrees of the Council of Trent

The most extensive formal declaration on Catholic beliefs regarding justification was produced by the Council of Trent. Martin Luther started the Protestant Reformation in 1517. The Council of Trent, held between 1545 and 1563, was as an ecumenical council under papal authority to deal in depth with the issues raised by the Protestant Reformation. The Sixth Session contains the statements essential for studying justification. The actual text of the decisions of the Council of Trent is available in book form and online.[6]

I recommend a firsthand reading the *entire* Decree on Justification in the Sixth Session of the Council of Trent. It will only take you a few minutes to read this important source in its entirety.

Be Cautious about Partial Quotations from Trent

As a pro-life leader, I know firsthand how distressing it is when the secular media makes you sound like a fool by slicing and splicing your interview comments into a foreign context. As much as I hated this being done to me, I must admit that as a Protestant minister I built my criticisms against Catholic beliefs by stringing together portions of a few out-of-context quotations. In fact, this is the most common method of making Catholicism look like a grotesquely false religion. The hearers of these distorted presentations shake their heads, convinced that Catholicism is in such deep error that a firsthand investigation of primary sources isn't worth their time.

Protestants who want an accurate portrait of Catholic beliefs should insist that when their preachers and teachers discuss Catholicism that they present an honest portrait and not a theological straw man. The only way you will know if you are getting a full and accurate picture of Catholic beliefs, particularly on grace and justification, is to read the above resources yourself. Otherwise, you'll fall prey to ministers such as my former self, having great sincerity, but misrepresenting Catholic beliefs.

The Epistle to the Romans

The theme of the entire Epistle to the Romans is justification by faith for both Jew and Gentile. This Epistle contains the most extensive expression of St. Paul's teaching on justification. It is the best book of the Bible, along with Galatians, to use when studying justification. Evangelical Protestants owe it to themselves to discover how Catholics interpret Romans and Galatians in full harmony with St. Paul.

The best way to get a beginner's exposure to a faithful Catholic interpretation of St. Paul is the *Ignatius Catholic Study Bible*. The study Bible commentary on Romans is available as an individual booklet, or as part of the volume on the entire New Testament.

Another method for getting a firsthand sense of how the Catholic Church understands particular passages in Romans and Galatians is to turn to the Index of Citations in the back of the *Catechism*. The Index lists the paragraph numbers in the *Catechism* where a specific Scripture passage is quoted or footnoted. Turn to these sections to see how the *Catechism* refers to passages from Romans and Galatians so critical for understanding justification.

What Have Catholics Said about the Importance of Justification?

The *Catechism of the Catholic Church*, quoting St. Augustine, says:

> Justification is the most excellent work of God's love made manifest in Christ Jesus and granted by the Holy Spirit. It is the opinion of St. Augustine that "the justification of the wicked is a greater work than the creation of heaven and earth."[7]

Like St. Augustine, St. Thomas Aquinas said, "The justification of the ungodly ... is greater than the creation of heaven and earth.[8]

A more recent Catholic theologian, echoing both St. Augustine and St. Thomas Aquinas, highlighted the importance of justification this way:

> The production of a single degree of grace in a single soul is a work superior to the creations of the worlds and of the entire universe. The justification of the sinner is the most important, the most wonderful, and the most touching of God's works, and the one that demands and reveals the greatest power and above all the greatest love.[9]

Catholic quotations like those above and the teaching on justification found in the genuine Catholic resources mentioned in this chapter can be an eye-opening experience for an Evangelical Protestant. I remember when I first started reading books about Catholicism written by Catholics. Previously, I had limited almost all my reading about Catholics to books written by Protestants. What a difference it made when I allowed Catholics to represent themselves. Proverbs 18:17 says, "He who states his case first seems right, until the other comes and examines him." Previously, I had unwisely made up my mind against Catholicism after hearing only one side of the story about this ancient Church. Hearing the other side of the story convinced me that this just might be the true Church founded by Jesus and continuing throughout history.

After a firsthand investigation of Catholic resources, you'll discover as I did that Catholics have preserved intact St. Paul's priceless teaching that salvation comes to us through the unmerited favor of God's grace.

What about Recent Ecumenical Statements on Justification?

This may surprise many, but my personal recommendation is that, unless you are a theological expert, you pass up recent ecumenical statements if you want to accurately understand Catholic beliefs on justification.

Motives energizing the various Protestant and Catholic ecumenical efforts over the past two decades are a cause for rejoicing. In our world that is rapidly abandoning Christianity, assaulting innocent human life, and descending into a dark age of hedonistic paganism, a united Christianity is needed more than ever. Therefore, authentic ecumenical efforts should be strongly encouraged.

The division between Protestants and Catholics began with a dispute over justification. It remains a major obstacle dividing them. Therefore it is fitting that recent ecumenical efforts tried to find common ground in the doctrine of justification.

Unfortunately, well-intended ecumenical efforts face a huge dilemma when creating doctrinal statements. In order to find common ground, such statements usually avoid theological precision in order to minimize the divisions that otherwise would become rapidly apparent. The ecumenical statements are usually crafted with deliberate ambiguities in order that well-intended harmony might be achieved. Unless you're a theological expert, you'll probably find the ambiguous theological statements extremely confusing. You could be puzzled further as you try to reconcile consensus statements in the main text of an ecumenical document that are qualified by critical points of divergence in an appendix.

Media reports of ecumenical discussions, even in religious periodicals, are not always a reliable basis for forming sound opinions. They may overly simplify the results by failing to take into account the limited denominations represented by Protestant signers, or the significant remaining points of divergence. Several media headlines conveyed the impression that the dispute over justification between all Protestants and Catholics is basically over. Not only is the dispute very much alive between most Evangelical Protestants and Catholics (see the Appendix I), but there is a considerable clash of opinions *within* Protestantism about the doctrine of justification.

In 2009, *Christianity Today* reported, "Over the past decade, justification has become one of the most hotly debated doctrines at conservative Protestant theological conferences."[10] The article claimed that "the long debate over how Protestants should view the Roman Catholic Church has received several jolts of intensity in the past fifteen years." The theological clashes within Protestantism referenced in this article include the years *after* the publishing of the 1997 and 1999 ecumenical statements on justification.

Therefore, it is inaccurate to say that the two ecumenical documents have healed the justification rift. Even the documents themselves admit that while progress has been made in understanding, serious theological and ecclesiastical obstacles still need to be overcome. For more about recent ecumenical statements on justification, see the Appendix I.

Many Evangelical Protestants are having second thoughts about Catholicism. They realize that countless conceptions they had of Catholicism were based on inaccurate stereotypes. If you find yourself in this group, then I'd like to offer some heartfelt advice. Your individual decision regarding your relationship to the Catholic Church isn't the same thing as a major ecumenical effort to unify Christians that have been separated for centuries. It is reasonable to expect that the reunification of Christianity might be a lengthy process. Yet, your decision to reunify with the historic Christian Church doesn't have to wait for decades of ecclesiastical ecumenical progress.

Considering the option of making the life-changing decision to become a Catholic is what is understandably left out of ecumenical documents. Remember that your decision can be made after you gain an accurate understanding of what the Catholic Church teaches.

In *Fidei Depositum*, his Apostolic Constitution on the Publication of the *Catechism of the Catholic Church*, Pope St. John Paul II mentions a dual ecumenical use of the *Catechism*: one for widespread ecumenical efforts of all Christians and the other for individuals who want to know what the Catholic Church believes.

It is meant to support ecumenical efforts that are moved by the holy desire for the unity of all Christians, showing carefully the content and wondrous harmony of the catholic faith. The *Catechism of the Catholic Church*, lastly, is offered to every individual who asks us to give an account of the hope that is in us (cf. 1 Pt 3:15) and who wants to know what the Catholic Church believes.[11]

I made my decisions about justification without the aid of the *Catechism of the Catholic Church*. It wasn't yet published when I was evaluating Catholicism, but how I wish it was. If you want a sure guide to knowing what the Catholic Church believes about grace and justification, then I repeat my advice to study the *Catechism* (paragraphs 1987–2029).

The Stumbling Block in My Journey toward Catholicism

From my own journey to Catholicism, I want to alert you to the harm that can be done by well-meaning, but less than fully accurate, Catholic authors on the topic of justification.

Catholic teaching on marriage and marital sexual morality opened my heart to a willingness to investigate Catholicism. Amazingly, many of the things in Catholicism I previously viewed as obstacles became attractions once I allowed the Catholic Church a fair hearing.

In the journey of most Evangelical Protestants becoming Catholic, few things are more critical than the questions about grace and justification. It wasn't easy understanding the Catholic view of justification. I had the natural tendency to try to understand Catholicism from within Protestant doctrinal categories and definitions. It turned out to be an impossible task since Protestants and Catholics use different sets of definitions and categories, leading to different perspectives and conclusions. Once I gained an understanding of the overall Catholic viewpoint on justification the details started becoming clear until ... I tripped over a stumbling block.

I was reading a book written by a nationally known Catholic apologist and published by a conservative Catholic publisher. I thought I was on safe ground until I got near the end of the book and read something that brought my pilgrimage toward Catholicism to an abrupt stop.

This Catholic apologist said he believed that Luther was right on the crucial issue of justification. He even expressed feeling guilt as a Catholic because his Church at the time of the Protestant Reformation was failing to preach the true Gospel.

I couldn't believe what I had just read. Here was a distinguished Catholic professor, lecturer, and apologist saying that Luther was the one who had the right beliefs on justification and that the Catholic Church was failing to preach the Gospel. He went on to exhort Protestants not to compromise on justification, or they would be adopting what St. Paul calls "another gospel." [12]

Had I totally misunderstood Catholic beliefs on justification after working so hard to understand them? I was stunned, perplexed, and confused. Fortunately, I had a knowledgeable friend, whom I could call for advice. He believed this author's statements on justification were inaccurate.

Just to be sure, I went back through the entire process of defining and clarifying justification both from a Protestant and a Catholic perspective.

In a way, I'm thankful God allowed me to go through this bewildering experience. It is one of the main reasons I've been interested in the doctrine of justification for the past twenty-seven years. You might say that the Catholic author who stated that Luther had justification right is responsible for this book. Encountering his claims taught me to verify all statements about justification by carefully comparing them with authoritative Church teachings. It was a hard but important lesson. I hope you can learn from my experience by sticking with the clear, accurate, precise, and authoritative resources recommended in this chapter for learning what the Catholic Church really teaches about justification.

Chapter Three

What Does the Term "Justification" Mean?

Both Catholics and Protestants believe that mankind finds itself in a state of sinfulness, that is, unrighteousness.

The eternal consequence of remaining in the state of unrighteousness is hell. Hence, the question "How can I become righteous?" is one of the ultimate questions every person needs to ask. Justification refers to how the holy God declares and makes unrighteous sinners righteous (i.e., justified) and thus heirs to eternal life.

Giving the Catholic view of justification of the sinner, the Council of Trent describes it

> as being a translation from that state in which man is born a child of the first Adam, to the state of grace and of the adoption of the sons of God through the second Adam, Jesus Christ, our Savior.

> This translation however cannot, since the promulgation of the Gospel, be effected except through the laver of regeneration [Baptism] or its desire, as it is written: Unless a man be born again of water and the Holy Ghost, he cannot enter the kingdom of God.[1]

Justification is the gracious saving action by which God cleanses us from our sins and makes us righteous.[2] This is the Good News of the Gospel.

The verb *justify* means the same as "make righteous," and the noun *justification* is synonymous with "righteousness." In the Greek New Testament, a single Greek word and its derivatives are translated into either of two English words, "righteousness" or "justification." Therefore, when you read the phrase "the righteousness that comes by faith," St. Paul is talking about "justification by faith."

In Romans 1:16–17, St. Paul states the theme of his Epistle: justification (i.e., righteousness) by faith.

> For I am not ashamed of the gospel: it is the power of God for salvation to every one who has faith, to the Jew first and also to the Greek. For in it the *righteousness* of God is revealed through *faith* for faith; as it is written, "He who through *faith* is *righteous* shall live."[3]

A Failure to Communicate

One of my all-time favorite movies is *Cool Hand Luke*, starring Paul Newman. The memorable line from the movie is uttered by the captain of Road Prison 36. After Luke is brought back to the chain gang, following an unsuccessful escape, the captain strikes him and says, "What we've got here is a failure to communicate."

There's also a "failure to communicate" between Protestants and Catholics when they discuss justification. A major reason Protestants and Catholics have difficulty understanding each other's perspective on justification is because they have differing definitions of justification. They both use the word *justification*, but with different meanings.

In my experience, Protestants often don't know that Catholics have a different definition of justification than they do. This includes many pastors, some "experts" leading anti-Catholic workshops, and even a few seminary professors. For example, after a public forum I gave on justification, a Protestant seminary professor accused me of "switching" definitions. I tried to explain to him that I wasn't "switching" definitions but that I was simply presenting *both* the Protestant definition and the centuries-old Catholic definition.

In fairness to this professor and others like him, I need to mention that I've also encountered Catholic leaders who mistakenly think that the Protestant definition of justification is the same one used by Catholics. You see, we do have a failure to communicate stemming from the confusion over the two different definitions of justification.

Definitions of Justification and the Resulting Interpretations of Romans

My fuller description of Catholic beliefs on justification appears in the Glossary. For now, in order to keep from getting overly complicated, I'm giving only partial definitions of justification.

Protestant definition of justification:

being *declared* righteous.

The word is defined narrowly in a way that separates sanctification and adoption from justification. Justification is a momentary act with on-going effects.

Catholic definition of justification:

being *made* righteous.

The word is defined comprehensively to include union with Christ, sanctification, and adoption. Cardinal Newman said, "The doctrine of justifying faith is a summary of the whole process of salvation from first to last."[4] Therefore, justification in the Catholic understanding shares with Protestantism a belief in a distinct beginning, but the Catholic definition includes the Christian's lifelong transformation.

The informative glossary toward the back of the *Catechism of the Catholic Church* gives this definition of justification:

> The gracious action of God which frees us from sin and communicates "the righteousness of God through faith in Jesus Christ" (Rom 3:22). Justification is not only the remission of sins, but also the sanctification and renewal of the interior man.[5]

Both Protestants and Catholics believe in justification, sanctification, union with Christ, and adoption. What Catholics view as the various aspects of justification, Protestants divide into distinct theological categories.

These differing definitions have huge implications for interpreting Romans and other Biblical texts pertaining to justification. Future chapters will pursue the question of the definition of justification in depth. But for now I'd ask you to ponder a simple, yet significant question: How much of an author's composition in any piece of literature is usually devoted to his theme? Even novice writers know that the main "parts" of any piece of literature need to be connected to the theme. If this is true about novice authors, why would St. Paul, when writing his most exquisite and theologically extensive epistle, devote just a few chapters to his theme and not the entire epistle?

Protestants use a narrow slice of Romans (chaps. 1–4) to understand justification, while Catholics use a much wider portion of the Epistle (chaps. 1–11). The overwhelming burden of proof lies squarely on Protestant shoulders to show why the justification theme of Romans 1:16–17 doesn't run throughout the theological teaching of Romans (chaps. 1–11).

Protestant and Catholics Outlines of Romans

Here are two outlines of Romans that show how the different definitions of justification might affect the interpretation of Romans:

A brief outline of Romans using the Protestant definition:

Theme of Romans: justification by faith (1:16–17)

I. The universality of sin (unrighteousness), hence the universal need for righteousness by both Jew and Gentile (1:18–3:10)

II. **Justification** (defined narrowly) **by faith *alone*** for both Jew and Gentile (chaps. 3–4)

III. Sanctification and adoption: separate and subsequent but arising from justification (chaps. 5–8)

IV. Jew and Gentile in God's saving plan (chaps. 9–11)

V. Practical exhortations, especially how both Jew and Gentile justified by God's grace should live harmoniously in the church at Rome (chaps. 12–15)

A brief outline of Romans using the Catholic definition:

Theme of Romans: justification by faith (1:16–17)

I. The universality of sin (unrighteousness), hence the universal need for righteousness by both Jew and Gentile (1:18–3:10)

II. **Justification** (defined comprehensively) **by faith** (chaps. 3–11)

   A. Justification by faith for both Jew and Gentile: baptism, union with Christ, sanctification, and adoption are included as aspects of justification (chaps. 3–8)

   B. Jew and Gentile in God's saving plan of justification by faith (chaps. 9–11)

III. Practical exhortations, especially how both Jew and Gentile justified by faith should live harmoniously in the church at Rome (chaps. 12–15)

In addition to the compelling reason that St. Paul's theme of justification should pervade his entire Epistle, there are other indications that the justification theme doesn't end with chapter 4. For instance, St. Paul explicitly mentions justification in Romans 10:4 and 10:10. These verses fall within the final theological section of Romans (9–11). I'll show in future chapters that St. Paul talks about subjects in Romans 5–8 organically related to justification.

You'll discover as we go through this study that the real difference between Protestant and Catholic beliefs on justification isn't that one believes the Bible and the other one doesn't. Don't accept such simplistic explanations. The real difference between Protestants and Catholics stems from differing definitions of justification (one narrow and one expansive) and thus *how much* of Romans should be used to form a doctrinal understanding of justification.

Even if Evangelicals don't agree with all the conclusions of this book, my hope is that accurately understanding the definitions of justification will promote clear communication and at least a respect for the Catholic use of Biblical texts in interpreting Romans.

The "Brief Overview" provides an outline of where the Protestant and Catholic beliefs on justification coincide and where they, in large part due to variations in definitions, are dissimilar.

Brief Overview of Protestant and Catholic Beliefs on Justification

How do unrighteous sinners become righteous (i.e., justified) so that they may inherit eternal life?

Protestant	Catholic
1. Our justification is by God's grace apart from works. The Protestant doctrine of justification is mostly similar to the Catholic belief regarding initial justification.	1. Our justification is due to God's grace. Our initial justification is without any type of works. (CCC 1996, 1998, 2003, 2010)
2. Faith alone	2. After initial justification, faith works through love, plus Baptism (gifts of grace).(CCC 1814, 1987, 1991–92, 1997, 2017, 2020)

Protestant	Catholic
3. A momentary act	3. An ongoing transformation, yet with a distinct beginning. (CCC 1987, fn.35; 1988–89; 1990; 2000) Only initial justification is a momentary act. Afterward the friends of God are able to increase the justice received. (Trent 6.10, Canon 24)
4. No "works" (connected to justification)	4. After initial justification, good works (by the power of the Holy Spirit) are necessary. (CCC 1813–15, 1991)
5. Justification is a legal declaration of "not guilty" (with no inward change)	5. Justification makes us inwardly righteous (not just declared righteous). There is a momentous inward change produced by grace. (CCC 1989–90, 1992, 1999, 2023)
6. Sanctification is distinct from and subsequent to justification	6. Sanctification (being made holy) is a vital part of justification. (CCC 1989, 1995, 1999, 2003, 2019)
7. Adoption is distinct from justification	7. Adoption and participation in Trinitarian life (i.e., sharing in the life of God) is a vital part of justification. (CCC 1813, 1996–97, 2021)

Chapter Four

Justification: By Faith, or by Faith Alone?

I s justification by faith *alone* as Martin Luther claimed and Protestants insist to this day, or is justification by faith—a living faith that isn't alone, but works through love?[1]

Remember that Catholics have a more expansive definition of justification that includes much of the Christian life. The Protestant definition of justification pertains to just the beginning stage of what Catholics call justification. Therefore, to accurately contrast the two views, the question should be, "How does the Protestant belief in justification compare to the Catholic belief in the first stage of justification?"

Catholics believe in justification by faith at the initial stage and justification by faith working through love during the remainder of the Christian life.

An inquiring Protestant might ask, "Do Catholics really believe in justification by faith for the initial stage of justification?" The Council of Trent definitively answered this question when it said:

We are ... justified by faith because faith is the beginning of human salvation, the foundation, and the root of all justification; without which it is impossible to please God, and to come unto the fellowship of His sons.[2]

Does St. Paul in his Epistle to the Romans say that we are justified by faith? Yes, multiple times. Remember that when an English translation of the Greek uses the words *righteous* and *righteousness*, it is referring to justification.

> For I am not ashamed of the gospel: it is the power of God for salvation to every one who has faith, to the Jew first and also to the Greek. For in it the righteousness of God is revealed through faith for faith; as it is written, "He who through faith is righteous shall live." (Rom 1:16–17)

> But now the righteousness of God has been manifested apart from law, although the law and the prophets bear witness to it, the righteousness of God through faith in Jesus Christ for all who believe. For there is no distinction; since all have sinned and fall short of the glory of God, they are justified by his grace as a gift, through the redemption which is in Christ Jesus, whom God put forward as an expiation by his blood, to be received by faith. This was to show God's righteousness, because in his divine forbearance he had passed over former sins; it was to prove at the present time that he himself is righteous and that he justifies him who has faith in Jesus. (Rom 3:21–26)

So far, there is perfect alignment between Catholic beliefs and St. Paul's repeated emphasis in Romans (chaps. 1 and 3) that justification is by faith. How does the Protestant belief in justification by faith *alone* compare?

We immediately encounter three significant problems. First, there isn't a single verse anywhere in the Bible that says justification (or righteousness) is by faith *alone*. Many people are led to believe that the Bible says justification is by faith alone when they hear something like the following: "We know that the Bible teaches justification is by faith alone as Paul says in Romans 3:28." The verse reference in Romans 3 is cited, but the verse itself isn't quoted. What does Romans 3:28 actually say? "For we hold that a man is justified by faith apart from works of law."

St. Paul rightly insists in Romans 3:28 that our justification comes to us by faith. Yet, he doesn't say that we are justified by faith *alone*. The Protestant insistence on the word "alone" is foreign to St. Paul. In the Greek New Testament, along with English translations, the word "alone" does not appear.

The second big problem with justification by faith *alone* is that the doctrine is explicitly refuted by Holy Scripture.

> You see that faith was active along with his works, and faith was completed by works, and the scripture was fulfilled which says, "Abraham believed God, and it was reckoned to him as righteousness"; and he was called the friend of God. *You see that a man is justified by works and not by faith alone.* (Jas 2:22–24; italics added)

Anti-Catholic polemicists are quick to criticize the Council of Trent's condemnation of the notion of faith *alone*, but the Trent they criticize is in complete agreement with St. James and St. Paul. Here's what the Council of Trent said about faith *alone*: "If anyone says that the sinner is justified by faith alone, meaning that nothing else is required to cooperate in order to obtain the grace of justification ... let him be anathema."[3]

In a paper on justification by an Evangelical seminary, the following commentary precedes Trent, Canon 9, cited above:

"Rome had officially ... and irreversibly, declared that the Gospel announced by the prophets, revealed in and by Christ, and proclaimed by the apostles, was actually heretical."[4]

This is a nice try at a grand slam against Catholicism, but it really is a swing at a straw man. The Council of Trent, precisely following Scripture, officially condemned justification by faith *alone*. It simultaneously affirmed justification by faith. If the Gospel really was by faith *alone*, why doesn't St. Paul mention it at least once and why does St. James condemn it?

Evangelical theologian R. C. Sproul rightly insists that the word "alone" was a foundational concept "on which the entire Reformation doctrine of justification was erected."[5]

I agree with Dr. Sproul that the Reformation's foundational belief in justification rests on the word "alone." Since Holy Scripture does not anywhere state that justification is by faith *alone*, the entire Reformation belief in justification is without any foundation in Scripture. This is the strangest of contradictions since Protestants insist that all beliefs should be based on the Scripture alone.

If justification by faith *alone* isn't found in Scripture and is refuted by Scripture, then how did the notion arise within Protestantism?

What you are about to read may sound too incredible to believe, but I assure you that knowledgeable Protestant theologians are familiar with the "alone" origin in Protestant theology. It is a chapter of Protestant history that many wish was forgotten.

When Martin Luther was composing his translation of the Bible into German he inserted the word "alone" into his translation of Romans 3:28. That's right, he just put it there, fully aware that it wasn't found in Greek and Latin manuscripts. To their credit, all modern Protestant translations of the New Testament into English don't follow Luther's brash act of adding words to Scripture.

"Wait a minute," you might say, "Maybe Martin Luther just made a slight mistake by inserting the word 'alone' into his translation." No, Luther knew exactly what he was doing. Though often missing from Protestant histories of the Reformation, here are his very own words on the matter:

> But as to you and our friends, I will give you my reason for using the word (*Sola*, alone) ... I knew very well that here, Rom.III., the word *Sola* is not in the Latin and Greek text, and it was not necessary for the Papists to teach me that. It is true, these four letters, S O L A, are not in it ... nevertheless, it expresses the meaning of the text; and if our German translation is to be clear and powerful, it ought to be put in.[6]

No one has the right to insert private notions into the sacred text. Yet, Luther used this tiny word "alone" as a wedge to justify splitting the Western Church in two.

You might be wondering what authority Luther imagined himself possessing that enabled him to make such a bold move. Again, Luther's own words are the most accurate testimony to his state of mind and heart:

> If your Papist makes much unnecessary fuss about the word [*Sola*], say straight out to him, Doctor Martinus Luther will have it so ... thus I will have it, thus I order it, my will is reason enough. For we will not be the scholars or the disciples of the Papists, but their masters and judges.

This is my answer to your first question; and as to their unnecessary noise about the word *Sola*, I beg of you not to give ... any other or further answer, but simply this much: Doctor Martinus Luther will have it so, and says he is a Doctor above all Doctors.[7]

In Luther's self-decreed infallible will, we discover the root of justification by faith *alone*. Remember our first test that seeks the belief adhering closest to St. Paul's teaching? Ask yourself, "Which is closest to the actual text of Romans: justification by faith *alone*, or justification by faith?"

Justification by faith *alone* isn't the language of the Bible. After five centuries of divisions stemming from Luther's insertion of the word "alone," isn't it time for all Christians to return to the authentic text of Scripture?

Enormous progress in ecumenical unity will result when Protestants unite with Catholics in affirming St. Paul's declaration that justification is by faith.

For I am not ashamed of the gospel: it is the power of God for salvation ... For in it the righteousness of God is revealed through faith for faith; as it is written, "He who through faith is righteous shall live." (Romans 1:16–17)

Chapter Five

What Happens When We Are Justified?

While living in Florida I experienced countless severe thunderstorms, many tropical storms, and a few brushes with hurricanes. I assumed that I knew all there was to know about Florida storms. Yet, all of these storms combined seem tame compared to the terrifying experience of the eye of a Category IV hurricane going over my home in 2004. Unless you've lived through one, you can't imagine the force of the devastating winds from a Category IV hurricane. It's an experience you'll never forget.

Digging a little deeper into the causes of tempestuous Protestant and Catholic conflict over justification is like my Category IV hurricane experience. The center of the storm in the justification controversy is the question: What happens to us when we are justified? This is where the stormy five-centuries-old debate on justification reaches its peak intensity, which remains to this day.

Imputed vs. Infused Righteousness

Protestant theologian Dr. R. C. Sproul rightly asserts that the distinction between imputed versus infused righteousness "touches the eye of the Reformation hurricane."[1] This is the point where extreme differences emerge between Protestants and Catholics.

Even the historic October 1999 Catholic–Lutheran ecumenical declaration on justification ran into a major difficulty at this very point.[2] The official response to the document from the Catholic Church emphasized that some theological differences were "aspects of substance" and not attributable to simple questions of "emphasis or language."[3] While it may be true that differences in language and definition are a significant cause of the debate over "faith *alone*" versus "faith with good works", simple differences with language and viewpoints are not the cause of the ongoing debate over imputed versus infused righteousness. We are dealing with two significantly different concepts.

The Vatican newspaper, *L'Osservatore Romano*, reported that the sharp differences between Lutherans and Catholics regarding imputation vs. infused righteousness was the principal reason the Catholic Church issued an official response to the Joint Declaration.[4] For Catholics, the interior renewal and sanctification of the justified person is "an essential doctrine defined by the Council of Trent."[5]

It's important to understand the meaning of these two terms which are often unfamiliar to the average Christian. It will be helpful for most readers to review carefully all the terms in the Glossary and to study the "Brief Overview of Protestant and Catholic Beliefs on Justification" at the end of chapter 3 before proceeding with this important chapter.

In a nutshell, imputed justification means "*regarding* (or *declaring*) us righteous," while infusion means "*making* us righteous."

While these definitions are overly simple, they enable us to begin learning the differences between these two important concepts.

Imputed Righteousness—the Protestant View of Justification

A summary of the Protestant doctrine of *imputed* righteousness follows:

- God is primarily viewed as a merciful judge.
- Justification is a legal declaration that sinners are "not guilty."
- Justification is an external act: a righteous external covering of the sinner with Christ's justice.
- Internally, justification leaves the person unjust and sinful.

Beginning with Martin Luther and continuing to our day, Protestants believe that justification is essentially a legal declaration, a judicial act. The easiest way to understand the Protestant view of imputation is to picture a courtroom. A guilty sinner is standing before God, the merciful judge, who pronounces the unrighteous sinner "not guilty."

In the Protestant concept of justification, the righteousness he receives is an external judicial decree. The sinner is not inwardly renewed, or sanctified, by justification.

Luther summarized his belief on imputation by saying that the believer is "at once sinner and just." By this he meant that the sinner stands externally declared righteousness, but internally he remains untouched by the righteousness of justification.

Some may puzzle over the concept of a divine declaration of righteousness (imputation) that leaves a person internally devoid of righteousness. They'd ask, "Isn't it an abuse of language to say that God declares someone righteous while he remains unrighteous inside?" When God spoke the universe into existence, his declarations had real effects throughout the cosmos. If justification is a greater work than the creation of the universe, as St. Augustine claimed, then wouldn't God's declaration of righteousness have tremendous grace-filled, righteousness-producing effects in the life of the believer?

Infused (Inherent) Righteousness — The Catholic View of Justification

The Catholic teaching of *infused* righteous can be summed up thus:

- God is primarily viewed as a Father.
- Justification produces a profound interior transformation— one becomes a "new man."
- The justified are cleansed from all sin (original and actual).
- The justified are infused with renewing and sanctifying grace.
- The justified are born anew as children of God.

Moving from the Protestant view of imputed righteousness to the Catholic view of infused righteousness, we move from courtroom to family room imagery. God the Father wants the justified to truly be his children. Therefore, he provides the grace for them to be internally cleansed from all sin in order to share his holy nature.

In Romans 4, St. Paul presents Abraham and David as examples of men justified by faith. What is the type of atonement (covering) for sin that David experienced? Psalm 51 is David's autobiographical hymn of praise for the comprehensive forgiveness and thorough cleansing bestowed by God's mercy. Ask yourself, "Did an internal cleansing coincide with divine forgiveness in David's life?"

> Have mercy on me, O God, according to thy steadfast love; according to thy abundant mercy blot out my transgressions.
> Wash me thoroughly from my iniquity, and cleanse me from my sin!...
> Behold, thou desirest truth in the inward being; therefore teach me wisdom in my secret heart.
> Purge me with hyssop, and I shall be clean; wash me, and I shall be whiter than snow. …
> Hide thy face from my sins, and blot out all my iniquities.
> Create in me a clean heart, O God, and put a new and right spirit within me. (Psalm 51:1–2, 6–7, 9, 10)

Essential to Catholic beliefs is that justification radically changes us from a son of the first Adam into a state of grace in the second Adam, Jesus Christ (Rom 5). This translation from a state of sin (unrighteousness) to a state of grace is called "adoption."[6] This is the act by which God the Father makes us his children because of the work of Christ. We will devote an entire chapter to the doctrine of adoption later, but for now it is critical to understand that infused righteousness is necessary for God's children to share a deeply personal relationship with their holy Father.

Once we are "in Christ" as St. Paul explains in Romans 5, we are brand-new people. Just how entirely new, St. Paul describes in 2 Corinthians 5: "Therefore, if any one is in Christ, he is a new creation; the old has passed away, behold, the new has come. All this is from God, who through Christ reconciled us to himself" (vv. 17–18).

Therefore, in justification we are not just declared righteous, we are made so. Catholic theologian Dr. Ludwig Ott writes, "It would be incompatible with the veracity and the sanctity of God that He should declare the sinner to be justified, if he remains in reality sinful."[7] St. Paul says, "For as by one man's disobedience many were *made* sinners, so by one man's obedience many will be *made* righteous" (Rom 5:19; emphasis added).

Catholics don't end their understanding of justification with Romans chapter 4. They include all of the following with justification:

- the translation from a state of sin in the first Adam, to a state of righteousness in the second Adam (Rom 5);
- the internal renewal, sanctification, and cleansing through Baptism (Rom 6);
- the new life in the Spirit (Rom 7–8); and
- adoption as children of God (Rom 8).

Hopefully, you remember the importance of an outline of Romans and how much of the Epistle you see as devoted to justification. Protestants view Romans 5–8 as teachings about a type of sanctification (making a person holy) that is separate and subsequent to justification. While Protestant theology separates justification and sanctification, Catholics beliefs join them as a simultaneous experience, just as St. Paul does in 1 Corinthians 6:11: "And such were some of you. But you were washed [referring to Baptism], you were sanctified, you were justified in the name of the Lord Jesus Christ and in the Spirit of our God."

In Acts 15, the first Church council met to answer the question about how Gentiles can be saved in the New Covenant. Did the Gentiles need to keep the Law of Moses and be circumcised in order to be justified? Peter arose and said:

> And God who knows the heart bore witness to them, giving them the Holy Spirit just as he did to us; and he made no distinction between us and them, but cleansed their hearts by faith. Now therefore why do you make trial of God by putting a yoke upon the neck of the disciples which neither our fathers nor we have been able to bear? But we believe that we shall be saved through the grace of the Lord Jesus, just as they will. (Acts 15:8–11)

Note that it was because of St. Peter's testimony that the Gentiles had been "infused" with the internal cleansing and renewing work of the Holy Spirit that the Council determined that God had justified them by faith, apart from keeping the Law of Moses. The evidence that the Gentiles had their "hearts cleansed by faith" was the basis for the early Church agreement that justification was by faith. What St. Peter testified to in Acts 15 and what the apostles affirmed is exactly what Catholics believe today: justification is by faith, and when God justifies someone he does so with a profoundly deep work of grace, forgiving the sinner and perfectly cleansing him from all stain of sin, and filling his soul with the life of divine grace.

One way to analyze the storm that still rages between Protestants and Catholics is as follows:

• The Protestant belief on justification by faith *alone* depends upon separating Romans 1–4 from chapters 5–8, which teach sanctification and renewal of the interior man.

• The Catholic beliefs on justification reflect an understanding of justification from an interpretation of Romans 1–8 (thus joining sanctification and renewal of the interior man with justification).

The two bullets above certainly don't account for all the differences between Protestants and Catholics, but they do help each side in the controversy understand how the Bible is used differently by each side in the justification debate in order to reach different conclusions. Protestants use a narrower portion of Romans to build their doctrine of justification, while Catholics use more of St. Paul's teaching to build a broader understanding of justification.

Infusion: The Indwelling of God Himself in the Justified Believer

When Catholics speak of "infusion," they are not talking about an inner jolt of cosmic energy. Rather, they are talking about the personal and glorious presence of the Holy God himself in the life of the believer. This astounding work of grace was foreshadowed by the divine presence in the Holy of Holies in the Old Testament tabernacle and temple.

The Holy of Holies was the special dwelling place of the infinite, awesome, all-powerful Yahweh, the covenant God of Israel. In this inner sanctum, the Creator of the universe would come to dwell and manifest his presence on earth. It was the distinguishing mark of the Israelites that the God of heaven would dwell in their midst.

The divine presence indwelling the Holy of Holies was an anticipation of a greater glory to come in the New Covenant. The Church corporately is now the special dwelling place of God in a way more profound than the tabernacle and temple in the Old Testament.

St. Paul wrote to the squabbling Christians in Corinth, sternly warning them that dividing the Church was a profane act, one that attempted to destroy the sacred New Covenant temple of God. "Do you not know that you are God's temple and that God's Spirit dwells in you? If any one destroys God's temple, God will destroy him. For God's temple is holy, and that temple you [plural] are" (1 Cor 3:16–17).

St. Paul also said in 2 Corinthians: "For we are the temple of the living God; as God said, 'I will live in them and move among them, and I will be their God, and they shall be my people'" (6:16). All Christians should forever be astounded that the Church is the special dwelling place of God.

The final aspect of the indwelling presence of God refers to the individual believer. Those justified are not infused by just an impersonal something, but by the holy presence of the personal God. This is a staggering reality.

When a person is justified, the sinful human heart is cleansed, purified, sanctified, and made righteous, thus making our hearts fit for the holy God to indwell. "Infusion" related to justification is when the glorious presence of God himself enters us as we individually become the temples of the living God. This is why St. Augustine said that the justification of the ungodly was a work greater than the creation of heaven and earth.

Every Christian should be conscious of the greatness of justification every waking moment. Yet St. Paul had to ask the Corinthian Christians: "Do you not know that your body is a temple of the Holy Spirit within you?" (1 Cor 6:19).

God's grace in justification doesn't leave us interiorly sinners. On the contrary, it touches our lives and transforms us in utterly profound ways. Divine grace transforms us into a new creation, a new reality, a new condition, a new temple — the dwelling place for the glorious presence of the Holy God.

What could be greater than the gift of God himself in the soul of man as a result of justification? The degree of glory in the justified could not have been foreseen by the most wise and powerful of the celestial hosts. The work of God's grace in justification dramatically exceeds every category of human and supernatural thought.

I realize that the Catholic doctrine of infusion of grace in justification is a point of controversy for many Protestants. Yet, with due reflection on this point of contention, you'll find that it is really a powerful reason to be drawn to Catholic beliefs.

Justification is more than an abstract doctrine about God issuing a legal decree. It is the priceless gift of God himself to the undeserving sinner. If God's grace is your "North Star," then ask yourself: "Which view of justification better exalts the grace of God?"

Chapter Six

Justification, Baptism, and Sanctification

Both Protestants and Catholics agree that St. Paul is discussing Baptism in Romans 6:

> Do you not know that all of us who have been baptized into Christ Jesus were baptized into his death? We were buried therefore with him by baptism into death, so that as Christ was raised from the dead by the glory of the Father, we too might walk in newness of life. (Rom 6:3–4)

Unfortunately, the recognition that Paul is describing Baptism is about the end of agreement. There is a bewildering variety of beliefs about Baptism among Protestants and between Protestants and Catholics. Evangelical Protestants vigorously disagree with each other about the mode of Baptism (sprinkling, immersion, pouring), the proper recipients of Baptism (believers only, infant Baptism, etc.), as well as the meaning and effects of Baptism.

Evangelical Protestants believe that Paul is discussing Baptism and the doctrine of sanctification in Romans 6. Most Evangelicals believe sanctification is a work of grace distinct but not separate from justification. Beyond this, there is widespread disagreement among Calvinists, Lutherans, Methodists, Holiness movement churches, and nondenominational Evangelicals over sanctification.

Catholics believe that sanctification is a vital aspect of justification. The Council of Trent said that justification "is not only a remission of sins but also the sanctification and renewal of the inward man."[1] Catholics believe that sanctification describes the effects of sanctifying grace, i.e., the righteousness infused with justification. The *Catechism* says, "The grace of the Holy Spirit has the power to justify us, that is, to cleanse us from our sins and to communicate to us 'the righteousness of God through faith in Jesus Christ' and through Baptism."[2] The *Catechism* then cites Romans 6 to show the Scriptural foundation for the belief that Baptism is what Catholics term the "instrumental cause" of justification.

Catholics also believe that there is also the lifelong process of growing in likeness to Christ, which is sometimes termed "second sanctification."[3]

Anti-Catholic apologists assert that Catholics have wrongly added sanctification to justification and incorrectly associated Baptism with it as well. Here's a word of caution: bold assertions don't always translate into proper interpretations of Scripture, especially declarations that neglect to explain accurately the beliefs they are trying to disprove.

The New Testament presents the doctrines of justification (i.e., righteousness), Baptism, and sanctification (Rom 6:1–23, Titus 3:5–7, 1 Cor 6:11) in a unified context.

Since Romans 6 is describing sanctification and Baptism in the continuing context of justification, then it is certainly sensible to view sanctification and Baptism in association with justification.

Romans 6 isn't the only place St. Paul writes about Baptism in a context with justification. In Galatians, the companion Epistle to

Romans, the themes of justification by faith, adoption (sonship), Baptism, and Abraham as the father of the faithful are found tightly woven in a single important passage (3:24–29):

> [24] So that the law was our custodian until Christ came, that we might be justified by faith. [25] But now that faith has come, we are no longer under a custodian; [26] for in Christ Jesus you are all sons of God, through faith. [27] For as many of you as were baptized into Christ have put on Christ. [28] There is neither Jew nor Greek, there is neither slave nor free, there is neither male nor female; for you are all one in Christ Jesus. [29] And if you are Christ's, then you are Abraham's offspring, heirs according to promise.

Is it a coincidence that both of the two Pauline Epistles dealing with justification (Romans and Galatians) have the themes listed below?

Justified by faith	Gal 3:24	Rom 3:22, 28
Not under law	Gal 3:25	Rom 3:19–21
Sons of God (adoption)	Gal 3:26	Rom 8:14–17
Baptism	Gal 3:27	Rom 6:1–11
No distinction between Jew and Greek	Gal 3:28	Rom 3:22
Abraham's offspring	Gal 3:29	Rom 4:16–17, 23–25

Those who might miss that Paul's theme of justification (1:16–17) embraces the entire doctrinal section of Romans (chaps. 1–11), can at least see the same themes joined in a single paragraph in Galatians 3. The doctrinal teaching in the Epistle to the Romans is in many ways an expansion of Galatians 3:24–29. Trying to view Baptism and sonship as distinct from justification in Galatians 3:24–29 ruptures the passage.

Romans 6 and Galatians 3 aren't the only places where St. Paul associates Baptism with justification. The baptismal "instrumental cause" of justification is also highlighted in Titus 3:5–7. The "washing of regeneration" in Titus 3:5 refers to the cleansing and sanctifying aspects of Baptism:

> He saved us, not because of deeds done by us in righteousness, but in virtue of his own mercy, by the washing of regeneration and renewal in the Holy Spirit [Baptism], which he poured out upon us richly through Jesus Christ our Savior, so that we might be justified by his grace and become heirs in hope of eternal life. (Titus 3:5–7)

The *Theological Dictionary of the New Testament*, considered by Biblical scholars to be one of the finest Greek reference tools ever compiled, says that the "washing" in Titus 3:5 and 1 Corinthians 6:11 (mentioned below) are clear references to Baptism.[4] Thus, Titus 3:5–7 is a perfect parallel passage to Romans 6, demonstrating that Baptism is indeed connected with justification.

Since the early centuries of the Church, the "washing of regeneration" has been understood as the new birth arising from Baptism. For example, St. Augustine said that the act of Baptism is "being washed in the laver of regeneration."[5] St. John Chrysostom, in his homily on Romans 6:5, said that Baptism bears the fruit of "righteousness [justification], sanctification, and adoption."[6]

Evangelical Protestants regard sanctification and Baptism as things separate and distinct from justification. They believe that sanctification *follows* justification in the order of salvation. However, 1 Corinthians 6:11 throws a monkey wrench into this supposed order since it combines all three actions while mentioning sanctification and the washing of Baptism *before* justification. "And such were some of you. But you were washed [baptized], you were sanctified, you were justified in the name of the Lord Jesus Christ and in the Spirit of our God (1 Cor 6:11).

The *Catechism*, in keeping with St. Paul in Romans, 1 Corinthians 6, and Titus 3, says: "The grace of the Holy Spirit has the power to justify us, that is, to cleanse us from our sins and to communicate to us 'the righteousness of God through faith in Jesus Christ' and through Baptism."[7]

In Romans 6, St. Paul emphasizes the believer's union with Christ as a result of Baptism. He said, "For if we have been united with him in a death like his, we shall certainly be united with him in a resurrection like his" (v. 5). Jesus Christ is the one who has merited salvation for those who believe. Christ's meritorious work is applied to us in Baptism since this sacrament joins the believer in a New Covenant union with Jesus.[8]

The *Catechism* calls Baptism "the sacrament of faith," conferring justification to the believer.

> Justification has been *merited for us by the Passion of Christ* who offered himself on the cross as a living victim, holy and pleasing to God, and whose blood has become the instrument of atonement for the sins of all men. Justification is conferred in Baptism, the sacrament of faith. It conforms us to the righteousness of God, who makes us inwardly just by the power of his mercy. Its purpose is the glory of God and of Christ, and the gift of eternal life.[9]

In summary, Catholics believe that justification is conferred by faith *and* by Baptism, in full agreement with the teaching of Jesus and Paul (Mk 16:16, Acts 19:4). We are not left internally unchanged by the grace of justification. Rather, the justified believer is thoroughly washed and made inwardly just.[10] As St. Paul describes in Romans 6, the old life is buried with Christ and a new internal source of life and obedience springs forth as a result of our being joined with Christ in newness of life.

There's still more good news about what happens when we are justified. Perhaps the most profound word in Romans 6 is the preposition "with." St. Paul repeatedly emphasizes that we have been united with Christ as a result of faith and Baptism. The *Catechism* expresses it this way:

> Grace is a *participation in the life of God.* It introduces us into the intimacy of Trinitarian life: by Baptism the Christian participates in the grace of Christ, the Head of his Body. As an "adopted son" he can henceforth call God "Father," in union with the only Son. He receives the life of the Spirit who breathes charity into him and who forms the Church.[11]

Justification does much more than pronounce us "not guilty." God's overflowing abundance of grace in justification transforms an undeserving sinner and then unites that person with God himself.

Chapter Seven

Adoption: The Crown of Justification

Thirty years ago I experienced a turning point in my spiritual life. I was reading a book entitled *Knowing God* by world-renowned Evangelical theologian J. I. Packer, when I came across these startling statements:

> You sum up the whole of the New Testament teaching in a single phrase, if you speak of it as a revelation of the fatherhood of the holy creator.

> If you want to judge how well a person understands Christianity, find out how much he makes of the thought of being God's child and having God as his Father.

> Our understanding of Christianity cannot be better than our grasp of adoption. The revelation to the believer that God is his Father is in a sense the climax of the Bible.[1]

At the time, I could easily rattle off the doctrine of the first person of the Trinity, give supporting Scriptures—even in the original New Testament Greek. With short notice, I could come up with a sermon on God the Father. Yet, I couldn't escape Dr. Packer's standard for evaluating a person's understanding of the New Testament. I had to admit to myself that God the Father really didn't occupy a vital and significant portion of my theological thinking and preaching. Was I missing something immensely important that was staring me in the face every time I studied the New Testament?

I dropped to my knees and prayed to the Father, asking him for light and understanding in the knowledge of himself. I wish I could say that illumination came within days, or even months, but it didn't. For me, getting to know the Father in the way Dr. Packer alluded to has unfolded gradually over the past three decades, often in surprising ways. In fact, the journey in knowing God continues to this day. Even though I'm still a neophyte on this expedition, I can testify that putting yourself on the path to knowing the Father is one of the most rewarding journeys a Christian can take.

"Abba Father"

So what does all this about God the Father have to do with justification and the doctrine of adoption? Before I give a more detailed answer, let me suggest a simple pair of Scriptural facts for contemplation:

1. There are only two books of the Bible that have justification as their theme: Romans and Galatians.
2. There are only two books in the New Testament outside the Gospels where "Abba, Father" is mentioned: Romans and Galatians.

Are the above facts just coincidence, or are they something which takes us to the very heart of what it means to be justified by faith?

An adoption "is the gratuitous acceptance of a person outside one's offspring to be one's son and heir."[2] Divine adoption is the inconceivably merciful and gracious acceptance of those justified into the divine family, thus sharing kinship with God the Father.

Protestant theologians, such as Sinclair Ferguson and J. I. Packer, give commendable emphasis to the doctrine of adoption. These men rightly state that adoption is the highest privilege of the justified, but they decry the frequent lack of emphasis within Evangelical Protestant circles. Yet these men, like other Evangelical theologians, vigorously claim that adoption is separate and subsequent to justification. I submit that making adoption something distinct and subsequent to justification is a principal reason why it loses emphasis in the lives and thinking of many Evangelicals.

In contrast, in Catholic doctrine, adoption is a vital component of justification, not something vaguely related, separate, and subsequent.

Trent's Brief Description of Justification

The Council of Trent's vitally important description of the work of grace in justification focuses on adoption:

> The justification of the sinner [is] a translation from that state in which man is born a child of the first Adam, to the state of grace and of the adoption of the sons of God through the second Adam, Jesus Christ, our Savior.[3]

This brief summary statement from the Council of Trent gets to the core of Catholic beliefs on justification. Notice that it highlights the process of justification as a transition from being "in Adam" to being "in Christ." This is a summation of Romans 5:12–21, where St. Paul emphasizes that justification places us "in Christ," that is, in a covenant union with Christ. What is the result of being in a state of grace as a result of justification? The answer is the unfathomable privilege of adoption as sons and daughters of God. Adoption is at the very heart of justification.

Certainly, justification includes the remission of sins so that we have peace with God. That is why St. Paul says, "Therefore, since we are justified by faith we have peace with God through our Lord Jesus Christ" (Rom 5:1). Yet this comprehensive peace with God is much more than a successful courtroom appearance before the divine judge.

Remember that the theme of the entire Epistle to the Romans is justification by faith for both Jew and Greek (Rom 1:16–17), not only chapters 3–4.[4] In Romans 5, St. Paul says that grace has transferred us out of Adam and into a union with the Second Adam: Jesus Christ. The emphasis falls on the abundant divine grace that has brought us into the New Covenant.

In Romans 6, St. Paul continues his teaching on the work of grace in those justified by faith when he says that being "baptized into Christ," joins believers in a covenant relationship that unites them "with Christ" and places them "in Christ."

In Romans 7 and 8, St. Paul contrasts the struggle between sinful passions of the flesh and "the new life of the Spirit" (Rom 7:6). From Romans 5 and 6, we heard that to be "in Christ" is a result of justification by faith. Now in Romans 8, St. Paul highlights the role of the Holy Spirit for those justified by faith and "in Christ."

Before looking at the role of the Holy Spirit in those justified in Romans 8, it's important to return briefly to Romans 5 and pick up the Holy Spirit theme when it is first introduced:

Therefore, since we are justified by faith, we have peace with God through our Lord Jesus Christ. (5:1)

God's love has been poured into our hearts through the Holy Spirit which has been given to us. (5:5)

In the same paragraph in which St. Paul states that we are justified by faith, he says that God's love has been poured into our hearts through the Holy Spirit (Rom 5:1–5). Something incredibly important is staring us in the face in these two verses. Rather than just stating the answer, I'll ask two simple questions to ensure that the answer remains at the forefront of your thinking.

Question 1: In Romans 5:1, whom do we have peace with?

Question 2: In Romans 5:5, whose love has been poured into our hearts?

"Father" is the one-word answer to both of these questions— a word that could transform your Christian life. It is so easy to read the word "God" in the New Testament and overlook that it is often a direct reference to God the Father.

In Romans 5:1, it is Jesus, the second person of the Blessed Trinity, who brings us peace with God the Father as a result of justification by faith. Burn this truth into your mind, and you'll know the heart of what it means to be justified by faith.

Life's Greatest Experience

In Romans 5:5, it is the Holy Spirit, the third person of the Blessed Trinity, who pours the Father's love into our hearts. There isn't a greater experience in all of human life than to have an infilling of the Father's love via the Holy Spirit. The human heart was made for this destiny of being a child of the Father. No pleasure, pastime, achievement, possession, or human relationship can begin to compare with the living knowledge of being an adopted child of the heavenly Father.

St. Paul could assume that a vibrant experiential knowledge of the love of God the Father was a normal part of the Christian life in the church at Rome. Christians today should seek such an experiential knowledge of the Father's love normative in their lives too.

In Romans 5, St. Paul introduces the subject of the Father's love being poured into the hearts of those justified by faith in Jesus Christ. In Romans 8, he expands the subject in one of the most important chapters in the Bible for understanding our relationship with God the Father.

The Goal of Human History

In Romans 8, we learn that all of human history is moving according to God's mysterious plan that predestines all things toward the goal of our "adoption as sons" (Rom 8:23). Even the physical universe "waits with eager longing for the revealing of the [adopted] sons of God" (Rom 8:19–20). When those justified by faith experience "the glorious liberty of the children of God" at the bodily resurrection, there will be a new physical universe for their eternal dwelling (Rom 8:21).

St. Paul describes the Christian life in Romans 8 as a life "in the Spirit." This new life in the Father's love is a result of justification (i.e., righteousness) by faith. He says to those justified by faith:

> [9] But you are not in the flesh, you are in the Spirit, if the Spirit of God really dwells in you. Any one who does not have the Spirit of Christ does not belong to him. [10] But if Christ is in you, although your bodies are dead because of sin, your spirits are alive because of *righteousness.*

11 If the Spirit of him who raised Jesus from the dead dwells in you, he who raised Christ Jesus from the dead will give life to your mortal bodies also through his Spirit who dwells in you. (Rom 8:9–11; emphasis added)

It is important to note that the word translated "righteousness" in Romans 8:10 is the same word St. Paul uses to express the theme of the Epistle:

For I am not ashamed of the gospel: it is the power of God for salvation to every one who has faith, to the Jew first and also to the Greek. For in it the righteousness of God is revealed through faith for faith; as it is written, "He who through faith is righteous shall live." (Rom 1:16–17)

In Romans 8, St. Paul isn't diverging from the subject of justification to talk about life in the spirit and adoption. Rather, he's showing that adoption by the heavenly Father is the pinnacle of justification. The Holy Spirit's assurance of adoption by the Father is proof that those justified really are God's children.

In Romans 8:14–17, we come to four verses worth their weight in gold.

For all who are led by the Spirit of God are sons of God. For you did not receive the spirit of slavery to fall back into fear, but you have received the spirit of sonship. When we cry, "Abba! Father!" it is the Spirit himself bearing witness with our spirit that we are children of God, and if children, then heirs, heirs of God and fellow heirs with Christ, provided we suffer with him in order that we may also be glorified with him. (Rom 8:14–17)

The Holy Spirit bears witness to our sonship in the depth of our being, crying out with us, "Abba, Father." Adoption isn't a wonderful add-on after justification. Rather, it is the pinnacle of the great work of justification by faith.

The Central Concept of Christianity

Anyone wishing to understand the Catholic teaching on grace and justification needs to grasp the central importance of adoption. Father F. Cuttaz, one of the finest Catholic authors on the subject of grace, shows that adoption is essential for understanding Christianity in its fullness:

> Our divine adoption is the central concept of Christianity, the truth to which all the others relate and toward which they all converge, the truth through which they become clear, and around which they are synthesized. All other truths flow from it as from their source, radiate from it as from their center, rest upon it as their foundation.

> God loves us as a Father and therefore lavishes upon us the most magnificent and absolutely gratuitous gifts, that is to say, supernatural gifts, above our nature, above its strength.

> The words Pater Noster [Our Father], that Jesus Himself placed at the beginning of the prayer He taught us, might well be engraved in golden letters over the portals of all our churches, to sum up and define what is taught in them and the substance and purpose of their religious ceremonies.

> God is our Father, we are His children. That is the whole of our holy religion. The reason Christianity is different from other religions and surpasses them infinitely is because it is the religion of the children of God, the religion of a God who is a Father. No other religion has ever dared to postulate the existence of such a love on the part of God, or such grandeur in man.

The Church is the society of the children of God. It is the great family of the heavenly Father.[5]

Certainly, Fr. Cuttaz meets and exceeds Dr. Packer's criteria for having a solid grasp of central New Testament teaching about having God as the Father of believers.

Many Evangelicals are suspicious of the Catholic doctrine of justification because they feel it may hinder a personal relationship with God. I held this very concern for two decades because of what I perceived to be Catholic teaching, but wasn't. Having now experienced Catholicism for two and a half decades, I have come to see that Catholic teaching on justification, with adoption by the heavenly Father at its heart, will lead a Christian to an ever-deepening personal relationship with the Triune God.

The Supreme Privilege of Adoption: Sharing in the Life of the Blessed Trinity

Throughout Romans 5–8, St. Paul uses manifold descriptions to communicate Christians' profound sharing in Trinitarian life as a result of justification:

With the Father:
> "we have peace with God [the Father]" (5:1)
> "we are children of God [the Father]" (8:16)

With the Son
> "in Christ" (8:1)
> "with Christ" (8:17)
> "fellow heirs with Christ" (8:17)

With the Holy Spirit

"in the new life of the Spirit" (7:6)

"you are in the Spirit" (8:9)

"you have received the spirit of sonship" (8:15)

The *Catechism of the Catholic Church* sums up justification by faith as an act of grace making us God's children and enabling us to share in the life of the Blessed Trinity:

Our justification comes from the grace of God. Grace is favor, the free and undeserved help that God gives us to respond to his call to become children of God, adoptive sons, partakers of the divine nature and of eternal life.

Grace is a *participation in the life of God.* It introduces us into the intimacy of Trinitarian life.... As an "adopted son" [the Christian] can henceforth call God "Father," in union with the only Son. He receives the life of the Spirit who breathes charity into him.[6]

Once our adoption as children of the heavenly Father becomes central to the question of grace in justification, then many of the Protestant objections to Catholicism should dissipate. Bringing adoption into an understanding of justification also answers our challenge question about which faith expression (Protestant or Catholic) best exalts the grace of God in justification. The Catholic belief in justification by faith that includes adoption exalts the grace of God to unimaginable degrees. This faith, once appropriated, gives believers the living realization in the depth of their being that they are children of the heavenly Father.

Evangelicals are known for their drive—a healthy and commendable one—to share with others how to have a life-changing personal relationship with Christ. I want Evangelicals considering

Catholicism to be aware that becoming a Catholic intensifies a personal relationship with Christ. The best term to describe what I've found about justification and salvation in the Catholic faith is "Evangelical Catholic."

Chapter Eight

Seeing "Good Works" through the Lens of Adoption

Most discussions on justification between Protestants and Catholics begin with a heated debate about works. The debate about the role of works boils down to this question: "Are any works necessary for justification?" Each side offers Bible verses in an attempt to defend respective positions. The result is often a stalemate.

Is there an overlooked perspective on the works question in justification that might break the Protestant/Catholic logjam that has dragged on for five centuries? I think there is, provided we approach the works question from the perspective of the Fatherhood of God and our adoption. As mentioned in the previous chapter, Catholic theologian Cuttaz shows how grace-filled vistas are opened to us if we keep adoption at the forefront of our theological reasoning.

> Our divine adoption is the central concept of Christianity, the truth to which all the others relate and toward which they all converge, the truth through which they become clear, and around which they are synthesized. All other truths flow from it as from their source, radiate from it as from their center, rest upon it as their foundation.[1]

Jesus taught us to call God "Father." The name *Father* in the New Covenant is as profound as the holy name of God revealed to Moses at the burning bush. Knowing God as Father is the Christian's holy ground. It is from the perspective of our relationship with God the Father that we should understand all aspects of justification, including the works question. As we grow in our knowledge of God the Father, understanding how works fit into a grace-filled view of justification is easy.

What happens when we view works relating to justification through the lens of adoption? For an Evangelical suspicious of any works related to justification, the entire notion of works is transformed in unspeakably great ways. Unfortunately, two profound changes have blurred our vision from seeing good works in relation to our heavenly Father.

The first change occurred at the Protestant Reformation. The Reformers didn't deny adoption, but when they separated it from justification, it had lasting practical effects on how we view our Christian life as sons and daughters of God. When justification is separated from Baptism (Rom 6) and adoption (Rom 8), Christians often fail to see how justification is directly related to our entrance into kinship with the Father and our Christian life as sons and daughters of God.

The second profound change arose as a result of changes in family life following the industrial revolution. For the past century and a half, industrialization caused a divorce between home life and work life. As fathers left home for the factory, or the corporate office, their children rarely saw their fathers work, let alone had an opportunity to work with them. For all of human history until the industrial revolution, sons worked with their fathers. Even with all the luxuries of modern life, an impoverished son is he who never has the opportunity to work with his father. Unfortunately, the concept of working with one's earthly father has become nearly a forgotten element in modern family life.

For the majority of his life, Jesus worked with St. Joseph in the carpenter's shop. Jesus was known in his hometown as "the carpenter's son" (Mt 13:55). In the carpenter's shop, Jesus learned carpentry through careful observation and imitation of Joseph. Today we would call this family-centered, on-the-job training. By the time of his public ministry, Joseph had died, and Jesus switched from working with Joseph to working with his heavenly Father. The Gospel of John shows Jesus following the same father-son training model he practiced in the carpenter's shop in observing and imitating the heavenly Father for his work in ministry.

> But Jesus answered them, "My Father is working still, and I am working." … Jesus said to them, "Truly, truly, I say to you, the Son can do nothing of his own accord, but only what he sees the Father doing; for whatever he does, that the Son does likewise." (Jn 5:17, 19)

When Jesus worked with his heavenly Father in John 5, was he engaging in forced labor as a slave, or internally motivated to work as a unique Son? The answer is as obvious as it is profound. "Jesus said to them, 'My food is to do the will of him who sent me, and to accomplish his work'" (Jn 4:34).

Slowly read the two sets of verses above because they reveal in the life of Christ the working-with-the-Father pattern that is to be reflected in the life of every Christian. There isn't a better picture of what it means for those justified and adopted to do good works.

At the heart of the Catholic doctrine of justification is adoption into a family-like kinship bond with God the Father. Catholics do believe that good works are necessary in the life of those justified by faith. These good works are not necessary for the initial step of justification, which is by faith. Yet, after entering into this relationship with the Father as an adopted son, the Christian is fully expected to follow the Father's lead in doing good works, just as Jesus did. A living faith works through love.[2]

In the Epistle to the Galatians, the companion Epistle to Romans, St. Paul soundly condemns the Judaizers, those false teachers attempting to get Christians, who were justified by faith, to put themselves back under the bondage of the Old Testament law. Trying to be justified by the works of the Old Testament law entirely nullifies the grace of God in justification (Gal 2:21).

In Galatians 4, St. Paul describes unaided human attempts to keep the precepts of the law as slave-like bondage. Such "works of the law" were incapable of enabling those bound by them to fulfill the law's demands. The Old Covenant pointed out the right thing to do, but failed to provide the power to do it.

Remember that the purpose of the Epistle to the Galatians is a robust defense of justification by faith. How does St. Paul describe our liberation from the bondage and slave-like service to the law in defense of justification by faith? Read carefully:

> When we were children, we were slaves to the elemental spirits of the universe. But when the time had fully come, God sent forth his Son, born of woman, born under the law, to redeem those who were under the law, so that we might receive adoption as sons. And because you are sons, God has sent the Spirit of his Son into our hearts, crying, "Abba! Father!" So through God you are no lon-

ger a slave but a son, and if a son then an heir. Formerly, when you did not know God, you were in bondage to beings that by nature are no gods; but now that you have come to know God [*the Father*], or rather to be known by God, how can you turn back again to the weak and beggarly elemental spirits, whose slaves you want to be once more? (Gal 4:3–9)

The transition from the Old Covenant to the New Covenant isn't from "works of the law" to no works at all. No, the transition is from the works of a slave to working with the Father as a son. What St. Paul condemns is doing the "works of the law" as slaves, and what he advocates is "faith working through love" as an adopted son (Gal 5:6).

There couldn't be a more profound difference.

Deprived Childhood?

I had the privilege of growing up on a farm. My father was a businessman, but he enjoyed outside work and thought working together would be a great way to raise children, so he and my mother purchased a farm. Some of my earliest and fondest childhood memories are working with my father on the farm.

One Saturday morning, my mother, feeling that I might be missing out on social excitement in the city, announced to me that she had arranged for me to go to a birthday party in town that afternoon. I immediately started bawling. Puzzled, my mother asked me what was wrong. Through my tears I sobbed, "I want to work with Dad!" To put it mildly, I was internally motivated to work with my father.

No, I wasn't a deprived child because of all the farm work. I was a very privileged son because I had extensive opportunities in childhood to work with my father. Perhaps our modern urban and suburban lifestyles have blinded us to a vital aspect of fatherhood, namely, working with children. Could it be that the work deficit in modern family life has obscured the vision of the high privilege of working with one's heavenly Father?

Freedom to Obey

At the heart of Pauline teaching is the truth that the New Covenant has brought a profound freedom to those justified by faith. Their new relationship with the Father gives them the willingness and the power to do his commands. The Old Testament law and covenant was holy, just, and good, but it lacked the power to work internal change in the human heart. Therefore, service to God in the Old Covenant often seemed like a form of slavery. At the heart of freedom in the New Covenant is an intense motivation to love and obey God. "For freedom Christ has set us free; stand fast therefore, and do not submit again to a yoke of slavery" (Gal 5:1).

Freedom to obey springs from the internalization of the law upon the human heart. Both Jeremiah and Ezekiel prophesied regarding the internalization of the law in the New Covenant.

> Behold, the days are coming, says the Lord, when I will make a new covenant with the house of Israel and the house of Judah ... this is the covenant which I will make with the house of Israel after those days, says the Lord: I will put my law within them, and I will write it upon their hearts; and I will be their God, and they shall be my people. (Jer 31:31, 33)

> And I will give them one heart, and put a new spirit within them; I will take the stony heart out of their flesh and give them a heart of flesh, that they may walk in my statutes

and keep my ordinances and obey them; and they shall be my people, and I will be their God. (Ezek 11:19–20)

The Heart Set Free

One of the leading English-speaking Evangelical Scripture scholars during the twentieth century was F. F. Bruce. The title of Dr. Bruce's book, *Paul: Apostle of the Heart Set Free,* written after a lifetime studying Paul, points to the essence of the Apostle's teaching:

> "Religion is grace, and ethics is gratitude."... For the gratitude which divine grace calls forth from its recipient is also the expression of that grace imparted and maintained by the Holy Spirit, through whom the love of God is poured out into the hearts of believers.... The gospel of free grace did not annul the essential law of God, but rather established it (Romans 3:31).

> Love is a more potent incentive to doing the will of God than legal regulations and fear of judgment could ever be....

> Paul certainly knew the love of Christ to be the all-compelling power in life. Where love is the compelling power, there is no sense of strain or conflict or bondage in doing what is right: the man or woman who is compelled by Jesus' love and empowered by his Spirit does the will of God from the heart.[3]

Dr. Bruce's description of the essence of Pauline teaching is in remarkable agreement with Catholic teaching. The glorious liberty of the sons and daughters of God is not a license to sin, nor is it a passive, do-nothing faith. Rather, it is the freedom to obey from the depths of a heart that has been touched by the Father's love.

The culmination of the work of God's grace in our justification, as described in Romans and Galatians, is being adopted by God the Father, being filled with the love of God the Father through the Holy Spirit, and exclaiming, "Abba, Father," as sons and daughters of the living God. Good works arise from filial obedience and love, not from a slave-like bondage to the law.

Misinformed Protestants assume that when Catholics insist on the need for works in justification that they are talking about "works of the law." Nothing could be further from the truth. As we discussed in chapter 1 above, the Catholic Church has formally condemned the notion of do-it-yourself salvation for more than fifteen hundred years.

This is how many Protestants are misinformed about Catholicism's emphasis on good works. First, it is stated that Catholics believe in "works" without distinguishing between "works of the law" and "good works." Second, Ephesians 2:8–9 is emphatically quoted—while conveniently ignoring verse 10, thereby inferring that Catholics believe in the type of works mentioned in verse 9. I wish I had a dollar for every time Ephesians 2:8–9 apart from verse 10 is quoted by someone promoting justification by faith *alone*.[4]

> [8] For by grace you have been saved through faith; and this is not your own doing, it is the gift of God—[9] not because of works, lest any man should boast. [10] For we are his workmanship, created in Christ Jesus for good works, which God prepared beforehand, that we should walk in them. (Eph 2:8–10)

The repeated assertions that Catholics believe in a type of Pharisaical "works of the law" method of earning your own salvation is patently false. The truth is that Catholics reject the type of works in verse 9 and affirm the good works in verse 10. The "works" mentioned in Ephesians 2:9 are the "works of the law" that can't save a person. Yet, a person saved by grace is certainly called to live a life filled with good works as described in verse 10.

Those wishing to reinforce further the inference that Catholics are promoting "works of the law" often quote Titus 3:5–7, yet they ignore Titus 3:8.

> [5] He saved us, not because of deeds [literally, "works"] done by us in righteousness, but in virtue of his own mercy, by the washing of regeneration and renewal in the Holy Spirit, [6] which he poured out upon us richly through Jesus Christ our Savior, [7] so that we might be justified by his grace and become heirs in hope of eternal life. [8] The saying is sure. I desire you to insist on these things, so that those who have believed in God may be careful to apply themselves to good deeds [literally, "good works"]; these are excellent and profitable to men. (Titus 3:5–8)

As a Catholic, I am amazed how many people fall for the Ephesians and Titus isolating-a-text-out-of-context trap. Then again, I must admit that this is a trap that I myself fell into, and I preached this misconception to others.

The Power for Good Works

A critical question pertaining to good works is this: "Where does the power to do good works come from?" If a Protestant or Catholic says, "I'm just trying to be a good person," that person is probably clueless regarding the source of strength for good works. Relying solely on oneself to live a life worthy of eternal life isn't doing good works at all, but an attempt at self-salvation.

St. Paul had zero tolerance for those who try to gain, or maintain, acceptance with God on the basis of Old Testament law-keeping, or human works unaided by divine grace.

The power to do good works comes from God. Such good works are a result of the work of God's grace in our lives. They should be called, "grace-works," since apart from grace we could never perform them. Since our Baptism, we are in a covenant union with God, who infuses deeply within us with grace to do his will. St. Paul expressed it this way: "But by the grace of God I am what I am, and his grace toward me was not in vain. On the contrary, I worked harder than any of them, though it was not I, but the grace of God which is with me" (1 Cor 15:10).

The Catholic faith teaches that Christians are dependent upon the grace of God for good works. Before, during, and after the performance of good works, the grace of God is at work. The Council of Trent, discussing the power to do the good works necessary in the life of those justified by faith, says:

> For since Christ Jesus Himself, as the head into the members and the vine into the branches, [Jn 15] continually infuses strength into those justified, which strength always *precedes, accompanies and follows* their good works, and without which they could not in any manner be pleasing and meritorious before God.[5]

This section from the Council of Trent refers to Jesus's teaching about the necessity to "abide in the vine" (Jn 15). The context of this passage is the Last Supper as Jesus is instituting the Eucharist (Lord's Supper) in the upper room. In this context Jesus says:

> Abide in me, and I in you. As the branch cannot bear fruit by itself, unless it abides in the vine, neither can you, un-

less you abide in me. I am the vine, you are the branches. He who abides in me, and I in him, he it is that bears much fruit, for apart from me you can do nothing.... By this my Father is glorified, that you bear much fruit, and so prove to be my disciples. (Jn 15:4–5, 8)

Catholics understand that New Covenant abiding in Christ is intensely Eucharistic. It is by sacramentally abiding in Christ that we receive the grace for the performance of good works. Apart from Christ, "we can do nothing." With Christ's grace, we can perform good works without burning out. St. Paul concludes Galatians with an insistence on the untiring performance of good works:

And let us not grow weary in well-doing, for in due season we shall reap, if we do not lose heart. So then, as we have opportunity, let us do good [literally "work the good"] to all men, and especially to those who are of the household of faith. (Gal 6:9–10)

In the Epistles of Romans and Galatians, the doctrine of adoption is the key to unlocking St. Paul's teaching about the Christian life of those justified by faith. A love-motivated service to our heavenly Father is what Catholics mean when they talk about good works in the lives of those justified by faith. It is also exactly what St. Paul teaches in both Romans and Galatians.

The Protestant and Catholic controversy over works and justification has churned on for five centuries. My hope is that an examination of works in justification in light of the doctrine of adoption might bring a significant measure of healing. Perhaps true and lasting ecumenical unity will begin with the heartfelt cry, "Abba, Father" (Rom 8:15, Gal 4:6).

Chapter Nine

Merit: Gracious Rewards from the Father

A month before joining the Catholic Church, I received a phone call from a family member urging me to engage in an hour-long dialogue with Dr. John Gerstner before finalizing my decision to become Catholic. Dr. Gerstner was known as a stalwart theologian in Evangelical Presbyterian circles. He was one of the staunchest Evangelical theologians opposing Catholicism.

I started our phone call by suggesting that we devote our entire hour to the doctrine of justification. Dr. Gerstner readily agreed. I stated that the Catholic Church does not teach that we are justified by "the works of the law" or "the works of the flesh." Dr. Gerstner acknowledged that Trent taught that justification is not by our unaided human efforts.

Next, I emphasized Trent's teaching that God's grace "always precedes, accompanies and follows … good works, and without which they could not in any manner be pleasing and meritorious before God."[1] Dr. Gerstner was also fully aware that the Council of Trent taught this.

I thought that our conversation was going surprisingly well— that is, until we started focusing on the topic of merit. I asserted that Catholic teaching on merit doesn't deny or obliterate the grace of God in our salvation. He said that any merit arising from good works completely cancels out grace.

I replied that merit couldn't cancel out grace since merit itself is a gracious act of God rewarding the divinely empowered good works of a person in the state of grace. How could a gracious reward for a work dependent upon grace deny grace?

I brought up the famous statement by St. Augustine, who said that when God crowns our merits he is crowning his own gifts.

The *Catechism of the Catholic Church* wasn't published at the time of our phone conference, but the preface to the Catechism's section on merit begins with a citation from the Roman Missal, which quotes this well-known statement of St. Augustine, the Doctor of Grace: "You are glorified in the assembly of your Holy Ones, for in crowning their merits you are crowning your own gifts."

Dr. Gerstner was adamant that any type of merit associated with justification nullifies grace. I responded by again asking, "How can a gracious reward to a justified person, based on a good work empowered by grace nullify grace?"

The bulk of our time together was spent going back and forth on merit. I asserted that merit was simply one of the aspects of grace in our salvation. Dr. Gerstner continued to stress that merit nullified grace. Dr. Gerstner was the perfect model of a Christian gentleman throughout our debate on justification. But at the end of our conversation, Dr. Gerstner warned me, in a manner as kind as possible, that I would go to hell if I followed through with my decision to become a Catholic and persisted in my beliefs on merit.

Looking back on our conversation more than twenty-five years later, I believe I made a mistake in under-emphasizing the framework of God's fatherhood when discussing merit in justification.

A friend, who had wrestled with similar questions on justification, suggested that I ask Dr. Gerstner, "Where in the text of Romans do we find the primacy of courtroom imagery?" Dr. Gerstner and I had briefly touched on the topic, but too quickly moved on to discuss justification without coming to any agreement on whether the courtroom or the covenant was Paul's basic context for discussing justification.

If God is mainly viewed as the judge in a courtroom, it is much more difficult to grasp Catholic beliefs on merit and works related to justification. On the other hand, if God is perceived primarily as a father reconciling his wayward children to his covenant family, then Catholic teaching on works and merit becomes easier to recognize as acts of divine grace.

Paragraphs 2008 and 2009 of the *Catechism* discuss merit in the context of God's fatherly action and as a result of our adoption:

> The merit of man before God in the Christian life arises from the fact that *God has freely chosen to associate man with the work of his grace*. The **fatherly action** of God is first on his own initiative, and then follows man's free acting through his collaboration, so that the merit of good works is to be attributed in the first place to the grace of God, then to the faithful. Man's merit, moreover, itself is due to God, for his good actions proceed in Christ, from the predispositions and assistance given by the Holy Spirit.

Filial adoption, in making us partakers by grace in the divine nature, can bestow *true merit* on us as a result of God's gratuitous justice. This is our right by grace, the full right of love, making us "co-heirs" with Christ and worthy of obtaining "the promised inheritance of eternal life." The merits of our good works are gifts of the divine goodness. "Grace has gone before us; now we are given what is due. . . . Our merits are God's gifts."[2]

Note from the paragraph above on filial adoption, that it is only the Christian justified by faith and in a state of grace who can receive merit from good works. Such a person is not striving as a slave, a servant, or a hired hand. His works and his rewards are those of a son working in collaboration with his Father. The reward of merit to the justified is the gracious reward of the heavenly Father to his children.

I can best illustrate the gracious reward of merit by recounting my experiences of family car washes. When my children were younger, I let them help me wash the family cars. Of course, their involvement made a simple, quick, and easy job complicated. Water fights not only sprayed the car we were working on, but also the car we'd just finished drying off. No matter how far away I put the drying rags, my children managed to get them wet too. Their hit-and-miss swirls meant that I had to go over all the areas that they had "cleaned." When it came time to clean-up our driveway disaster, they managed to disappear, heading inside for a bath and a change into dry clothes. The amazing thing is that after all of this I often paid my children a small reward for their work. Believe me, this pay was a gracious reward.

I don't want to repeat in this book the mistake I made with Dr. Gerstner—namely, underemphasizing God's fatherhood and our adoption as sons and daughters as the key to understanding all aspects of justification.

The endless disputes about works and merit in justification stem, in large measure, from two different conceptions of God's role in our salvation. Do we perceive him as the judge in a courtroom, or as the father in St. Luke's parable of the prodigal son? Good works and meritorious rewards easily fit into a belief system of salvation by grace, provided God's fatherhood is kept in focus.

It's difficult to escape the New Testament's repeated promises of reward to the faithful. Here is a sampling:

Rejoice and be glad, for your reward is great in heaven. (Mt 5:12)

Jesus said to them, "Truly, I say to you ... every one who has left houses or brothers or sisters or father or mother or children or lands, for my name's sake, will receive a hundredfold, and inherit eternal life. (Mt 19:28–30)

For truly, I say to you, whoever gives you a cup of water to drink because you bear the name of Christ, will by no means lose his reward. (Mk 9:41)

For he will render to every man according to his works: to those who by patience in well-doing seek for glory and honor and immortality, he will give eternal life; but for those who are factious and do not obey the truth, but obey wickedness, there will be wrath and fury.... For it is not the hearers of the law who are righteous before God, but the doers of the law who will be justified. (Rom 2:6–8, 13)

I planted, Apollos watered, but God gave the growth. So neither he who plants nor he who waters is anything, but only God who gives the growth. He who plants and he who waters are equal, and each shall receive his wages according to his labor. (1 Cor 3:6–8)

Whatever your task, work heartily, as serving the Lord and not men, knowing that from the Lord you will receive the inheritance as your reward; you are serving the Lord Christ. (Col 3:23–24)

Whatever good any one does, he will receive the same again from the Lord. (Eph 6:8)

And without faith it is impossible to please him. For whoever would draw near to God must believe that he exists and that he rewards those who seek him. (Heb 11:6)

For God is not so unjust as to overlook your work and the love which you showed for his sake in serving the saints, as you still do. (Heb 6:10)

With these Scriptures in mind, it's preposterous to assert that believing God will graciously reward his children results in a person being sent to hell.

God the Father, like any good father, allows his children to work with and for him. Grace-filled works and gracious merit don't nullify a covenant relationship. Rather, they are rich blessings stemming from covenant life with the Father. This family work is the farthest thing in the world from the works of a slave or non-family wage-earner expecting reward. Family work is actively sharing in the love of God:

> *The charity of Christ is the source in us of all our merits* before God. Grace, by uniting us to Christ in active love, ensures the supernatural quality of our acts and consequently their merit before God and before men. The saints have always had a lively awareness that their merits were pure grace.[3]

Family work is a significant way in which any father incorporates a son into his life. In like fashion, it is the heavenly Father's gracious love that allows us to work with him. God's sovereignty isn't jeopardized when his goodness condescends to incorporate his children in his work. "God is the sovereign master of his plan. But to carry it out he also makes use of his creatures' cooperation. This use is not a sign of weakness, but rather a token of almighty God's greatness and goodness."[4]

When the Father rewards this work, he is piling grace upon grace to overwhelming degrees. Does this amount of superabundant grace lavished upon us shock you? It should. Even the angels are astonished at the extremes of God's glorious grace in choosing, redeeming, justifying, and rewarding us.

It's ironic that some of those who so earnestly seek to safeguard God's grace deny the grace of meritorious rewards for the justified. The fullness of the Christian faith magnifies God's grace in *every* aspect of salvation—including the gracious rewards for grace-empowered works. Yes, it always needs to be remembered that initial justification is impossible to merit. Yet, if we want to magnify divine grace throughout the Christian life, then we can't amputate any facet of it.

Chapter Ten

Can I Lose My Justification?

E vangelicals often ask Catholics, "Do you really believe that justification can be lost?" The answer depends upon what one means by "lost."

Catholics do *not* believe that justification is lost through inadvertent acts. Losing justification is not like losing your car keys, cell phone, or television remote. Catholics do not believe one can lose one's justification by unconscious slips or unintentional acts.

There is a Catholic belief that a person can lose his justification through a conscious, willful, and gravely sinful act. I fully realize that Evangelicals hearing this in the abstract think this seems outrageous. The passionate Evangelical response is usually, "What about the promises of Jesus the Good Shepherd to never let anyone snatch a believer out of his and the Father's hands (Jn 10:28–29)?"

Both Catholics and Protestants believe that God will provide sufficient grace to endure any temptation and every persecution.

> No temptation has overtaken you that is not common to man. God is faithful, and he will not let you be tempted beyond your strength, but with the temptation will also provide the way of escape, that you may be able to endure it. (1 Cor 10:13)

St. Paul promised Christians in Rome that even suffering the most unimaginable forms of persecution would not be able to separate believers from God the Father and Jesus his Son (Rom 8). A little over a decade after Paul penned the Epistle to the Romans, imperial persecution broke out in Rome. Paul's promise of the Good Shepherd's care was severely tested for two and a half centuries. Despite the Coliseum and hideous persecutions throughout the empire, nothing was able to separate Christians from Christ, or snatch them out of the Father's hand.

Returning to the big question, "Can justification be lost through willful and serious sin?" There are varieties (and subvarieties) of Protestant answers to this question. Some Protestants believe that it is utterly impossible to lose one's salvation; others believe that it can be lost only through unbelief, while still others believe that professing Christians who turn to a life of sin were never really saved to begin with.

Catholics answer the big question in the affirmative, believing that not only unbelief, but by every mortal sin, justification is lost. Catholics define a mortal sin as a "grave matter ... committed with full knowledge and deliberate consent."[1]

Ezekiel provides the clearest and sternest warning to those who imagine that turning from righteousness to sin has no consequences (remember that the word *righteousness* is an alternative expression for the justice in justification):

> But if a wicked man turns away from all his sins which he has committed and keeps all my statutes and does what is lawful and right, he shall surely live; he shall not die. None of the transgressions which he has committed shall be remembered against him; for the righteousness which he has done he shall live. Have I any pleasure in the death

of the wicked, says the Lord God, and not rather that he should turn from his way and live? But when a righteous man turns away from his righteousness and commits iniquity and does the same abominable things that the wicked man does, shall he live? None of the righteous deeds which he has done shall be remembered; for the treachery of which he is guilty and the sin he has committed, he shall die.

Yet you say, "The way of the Lord is not just." Hear now, O house of Israel: Is my way not just? Is it not your ways that are not just? When a righteous man turns away from his righteousness and commits iniquity, he shall die for it; for the iniquity which he has committed he shall die. Again, when a wicked man turns away from the wickedness he has committed and does what is lawful and right, he shall save his life. Because he considered and turned away from all the transgressions which he had committed, he shall surely live, he shall not die.…

Therefore I will judge you, O house of Israel, every one according to his ways, says the Lord God. Repent and turn from all your transgressions, lest iniquity be your ruin. (Ezek 18:21–28, 30)

God repeats his dire warning to the righteous who turn from their righteousness in Ezekiel 33:12–20. Don't fall for the temptation to blow off Ezekiel's solemn warnings by saying that it's Old Testament stuff that belongs to another dispensation. St. Paul told the Corinthian Christians that the judgment that fell upon Israel was a warning for those in the New Covenant:

Nevertheless with most of them God was not pleased; for they were overthrown in the wilderness. Now these things are warnings for us, not to desire evil as they did.… We must not indulge in immorality as some of them did, and twenty-three thousand fell in a single day. We must not put the Lord to the test, as some of them did and were destroyed by serpents; nor grumble, as some of them did and were destroyed by the Destroyer. Now these things happened to them as a warning, but they were written down for our instruction, upon whom the end of the ages has come. Therefore let any one who thinks that he stands take heed lest he fall. (1 Cor 10:5–6, 8–12)

It misconstrues St. Paul's teaching to assert that justification by faith is a once-for-all ticket allowing a person to live in serious, unrepentant sin without consequences. In Galatians, one of the justification Epistles, St. Paul warns Christians:

Now the works of the flesh are plain: immorality, impurity, licentiousness, idolatry, sorcery, enmity, strife, jealousy, anger, selfishness, dissension, party spirit, envy, drunkenness, carousing, and the like. I warn you, as I warned you before, that those who do such things shall not inherit the kingdom of God. (Gal 5:19–21)

St. Peter takes the warning to wayward Christians a step further by asserting that it would have been better never to have known Christ than for a baptized believer to fall back into a life of sin:

Uttering loud boasts of folly, they entice with licentious passions of the flesh men who have barely escaped from those who live in error. They promise them freedom, but they themselves are slaves of corruption; for whatever overcomes a man, to that he is enslaved. For if, after they have escaped the defilements of the world through the knowledge of our Lord and Savior Jesus Christ, they are again entangled in them and overpowered, *the last state has become worse for them than the first. For it would have been better for them never to have known the way of righteousness than after knowing it to turn back from the holy commandment delivered to them.* It has happened to them according to the true proverb, The dog turns back to his own vomit, and the sow is washed only to wallow in the mire. (2 Pet 2:18–22; emphasis added)

Just beginning a life of faith is inadequate for inheriting eternal life. To inherit eternal life, Christians must continue in faithfulness to the end of their lives. Those who attempt to circumvent this teaching using verses from St. Paul should heed what the Apostle said about himself:

Do you not know that in a race all the runners compete, but only one receives the prize? So run that you may obtain it. Every athlete exercises self-control in all things. They do it to receive a perishable wreath, but we an imperishable. Well, I do not run aimlessly, I do not box as one beating the air; but I pommel my body and subdue it, lest after preaching to others I myself should be disqualified. (1 Cor 9:24–27)

A major theme of the Epistle to the Hebrews is the need for perseverance. Christians are explicitly warned against falling away and told that they need to persevere to the end of their lives:

Take care, brethren, lest there be in any of you an evil, unbelieving heart, leading you to fall away from the living God. But exhort one another every day, as long as it is called "today," that none of you may be hardened by the deceitfulness of sin. For we share in Christ, if only we hold our first confidence firm to the end. (Heb 3:12–14)

For you have need of endurance, so that you may do the will of God and receive what is promised.

"For yet a little while,
and the coming one shall come and shall not tarry;

> but my righteous one shall live by faith,
> and if he shrinks back,
> my soul has no pleasure in him."

But we are not of those who shrink back and are destroyed, but of those who have faith and keep their souls. (Heb 10:36–39)

Protestant systematic theology asserts that justification is a once-and-for-all event. Once a person exercises saving faith in Jesus, then it is claimed that they are forever unconditionally justified. In stark contrast to this assertion is Jesus's solemn warning that there is a final justification, or condemnation, based on what was said throughout a person's lifetime. "I tell you, on the day of judgment men will render account for every careless word they utter; for by your words you will be justified, and by your words you will be condemned" (Mt 12:36–37).

In the final book of the Bible (Revelation 2–3), Jesus sternly rebukes the false teaching corrupting the early Church. These false prophets promised Christians that they could engage in grave sin and still be assured of good standing with God. The Epistles of Second Peter and Jude condemn this same type of teaching that perverted "the grace of our God into licentiousness" (Jude 4).

The Book of Revelation concludes with Jesus giving a solemn warning that God will exclude all evildoers from the New Jerusalem. No matter what you may have read or heard from respected leaders, *all* persistent evildoers are outside the eternal city.

> "Let the evildoer still do evil, and the filthy still be filthy,
> and the righteous still do right, and the holy still be holy."

"Behold, I am coming soon, bringing my recompense, to repay every one for what he has done. I am the Alpha and the Omega, the first and the last, the beginning and the end."

Blessed are those who wash their robes, that they may have the right to the tree of life and that they may enter the city by the gates. Outside are the dogs and sorcerers and fornicators and murderers and idolaters, and every one who loves and practices falsehood. (Rev 22:11–15)

The next verse declares that the message of Revelation is a "testimony for the churches." The final promise and warning aren't for the "other guys"— they are for Christians.

Some Evangelicals may find Jesus's words at the end of Revelation difficult to harmonize with what they have been taught about St. Paul's teaching in Romans and Galatians. The difficulty stems from neglecting some easy-to-understand but difficult-to-digest words from St. Paul that harmonize perfectly with Revelation 22:11–15.

Do you suppose, O man, that when you judge those who do such things and yet do them yourself, you will escape the judgment of God? Or do you presume upon the riches of his kindness and forbearance and patience? Do you not know that God's kindness is meant to lead you to repentance? But by your hard and impenitent heart you are storing up wrath for yourself on the day of wrath when God's righteous judgment will be revealed. For he will render to every man according to his works: to those who by patience in well-doing seek for glory and honor and immortality, he will give eternal life; but for those who are factious and do not obey the truth, but obey wickedness, there will be wrath and fury. (Rom 2:3–8)

Despite all of these Scriptures describing the possibility of losing one's eternal salvation, the teaching is still offensive to most Evangelical ears. Is there a framework by which Evangelicals can understand Catholic teaching on this difficult aspect of justification? I believe the fatherhood of God points the way.

I've already highlighted the need to be aware of God's fatherhood and our adoption as the perspective necessary to understand Catholic teaching on justification. Nowhere is this more important than in examining the question about losing justification. In order to understand how justification can be lost, we need to take a second look at the Council of Trent's brief summary of justification to see how justification is accomplished.

> The justification of the sinner [is] a translation from that state in which man is born a child of the first Adam, to the state of grace and of the adoption of the sons of God through the second Adam, Jesus Christ, our Savior.[2]

Justification entails our transfer from a state of sin to a state of grace and adoption as sons of the heavenly Father. Therefore, justification is that state of grace as adopted sons of God the Father. With this in our minds, we are ready to understand how and why justification can be lost by asking a simple question: "Will the Father allow one of his sons to leave home (i.e., the covenant family)?" For anyone who has read the parable of the prodigal son in Luke 15, the answer is obvious.

At its ultimate root, sin is a willful turning away from the love of God the Father. Pope St. John Paul II even went so far as to suggest that God's fatherhood and mankind's turning from him is the key to interpreting all of reality:

The father-son paradigm is ageless. It is older than human history. The "rays of fatherhood" contained in this formulation belong to the Trinitarian Mystery of God Himself, which shines forth from Him, illuminating man and his history.

This notwithstanding, as we know from Revelation, in human history the "rays of fatherhood" meet a first resistance in the obscure but real fact of original sin. *This is truly the key for interpreting reality.* Original sin is not only the violation of a positive command of God but also, and above all, a violation of *the will of God as expressed in that command. Original sin attempts, then, to abolish fatherhood,* destroying its rays which permeate the created world, placing in doubt the truth about God who is Love and leaving man only with a sense of the master-slave relationship.[3]

God the Father doesn't force or compel his children to remain in a covenant relationship with himself. If they willfully turn from him in mortal sin, he allows them to have their way since it's not by law, or compulsion, that we stay in a relationship with the Father. This is the frightening freedom that love requires.

Evangelicals may be unfamiliar with what Catholics believe about mortal sin. Here is how the *Catechism* explains it:

Mortal sin [is] a grave infraction of the law of God that destroys the divine life in the soul of the sinner (sanctifying grace), constituting a turn away from God. For a sin to be mortal, three conditions must be present: grave matter, full knowledge of the evil of the act, and full consent of the will.[4]

Catholics understand St. John's contrasting a "deadly sin" with "what is not a deadly sin" (see 1 Jn 5:16–17, RSV2CE), as distinguishing between the grievous type of sin that is "mortal" (forfeiting the life of Christ) and a sin which is "venial" (a more minor offense against God, or a sin committed without full consent of the will).[5]

What happens to those deliberately rejecting the Father's will by committing a grave sin with full knowledge and consent of their will? If they lose their justification by gravely sinful acts, can they recover their lost justification? The answer is always yes, provided that they do it within their lifetime. The sacrament of Penance is how justification is recovered and a relationship with the heavenly Father is restored. The sacrament of Penance is like a reenactment of the prodigal son returning to the Father. The repentant are always welcomed home by the loving embrace of the Father.

A covenant life in union with God the Father is always possible. God's grace provides strength to love, obey, and follow him. When his children stumble, he offers mercy, forgiveness, and restoration. The heavenly Father provides abundant grace to his children in manifold ways, but most particularly through the sacraments. The *Catechism of the Catholic Church* identifies the Father as the source and goal of the sacraments and liturgy.[5] While preparing for the liturgy, "the grace of the Holy Spirit seeks to awaken faith, conversion of heart, and adherence to the Father's will."[6]

God will faithfully provide the power, the grace, and the internal motivation to live as his children through the sacraments and the other means of grace. This assurance is extended to everyone seeking to love and honor the heavenly Father and his Son, Jesus Christ.

Chapter Eleven

New Perspectives on St. Paul

For the past three to four decades, there has been growing interest among Biblical scholars in what is termed the "New Perspective on Paul." Some of the leading figures in this movement are the Protestant scholars E. P. Sanders, N. T. Wright, and James D. G. Dunn.[1] Many contemporary Pauline scholars have abandoned traditional interpretations of St. Paul's Epistles and replaced them with varying viewpoints from the New Perspective. In all probability, we are at the beginning phases of a sea-change in Pauline studies that will reverberate in Biblical studies for generations to come.

Throughout the earlier chapters in this book, I've mainly used the traditional interpretations of St. Paul's Epistles when describing Protestant beliefs and contrasting them with Catholicism. The primary reason for using the traditional perspective is that most laymen at this time have only minimal exposure to the New Perspective. It's my opinion that some variety of the New Perspective will gain wide popular acceptance in the future. Yet my purpose in writing this book is to help people who are wrestling with the justification questions *now*. Therefore, in order to provide timely assistance, I used the traditional interpretations of Paul. It will not only take time for the New Perspective to gain popular understanding and acceptance, but the New Perspective itself will grow through several stages of refinement.

If reading this book using the traditional understanding of St. Paul has settled the Catholic justification issues for you, then your acceptance of the New Perspective in the future should not unsettle any conclusions you've reached. The reason is that if you accept the central tenets of the New Perspective, then you will find it even easier to accept Catholic teaching on justification. The bottom line is that the Catholic case for justification can stand using either the traditional perspective on St. Paul, or the new one.

A significant cause of Evangelical opposition to the New Perspective arises out of a fear that several implications of this new movement lead toward Rome. Yet more fundamental than this fear, is the question of whether or not the New Perspective leads to a more accurate interpretation of St. Paul's Epistles. For any Christian committed to pursuing the truth, the question should focus on whether the New Perspective is true, regardless of where it leads. A knee-jerk reaction against a deeper understanding of Scripture cannot be justified just because it may remove some of the barriers against Catholicism.

In private conversations, it has been reported to me that in some quarters the opposition to the New Perspective resembles a witch hunt, especially for those seeking ordination in some Evangelical Protestant denominations. Trying to erect a Maginot Line against the New Perspective will fail miserably. Seminarians and serious laymen are not impressed by leaders and professors who are unwilling to engage intellectually and doctrinally a position that seems to make better sense out of Scripture texts.

At a minimum, the traditional view of Paul's Epistles will need to be informed and modified as a result of the more accurate understanding of first-century Judaism at the basis of the New Perspective. After five centuries, the Reformation's views on justification are being challenged in significant ways by the New Perspective—a movement within Pauline studies that started with Protestant scholars.

The New Perspective is almost certain to be a main topic of Pauline studies throughout the twenty-first century. The body of published literature on the New Perspective is already significant and is showing no sign of slowing down. In addition to published materials, there are on the Internet substantial resources and serious debates on the New Perspective. In this brief chapter, I can outline only a few of the major themes from the New Perspective and relate some of the implications for understanding justification.

What Is the New Perspective on Paul?

The New Perspective on St. Paul has emerged as a result of a significant advance in the historical understanding of first-century Judaism— the religious and cultural environment to which Paul was deeply attached before his conversion.

The primary historical question raised by the New Perspective is, "Did first-century Judaism teach that a legalistic works-righteousness was necessary for *entering* a saving covenant relationship with Yahweh?" If the answer is no, then a new perspective on St. Paul's message in Romans and Galatians emerges. The new perspective in turn fundamentally alters the classical debate on justification between Protestants and Catholics.

The traditional perspective believes that Judaism at the time of Jesus and Paul taught the necessity of human works in order to earn salvation (i.e., works-righteousness for gaining salvation). Martin Luther believed that the Catholic Church in his day was basically a revival of first-century Judaism's works-righteousness.

I've already shown that the Catholic Church never taught that we earn our justification by unaided human works but rather officially declared the notion a heresy. The New Perspective has convincingly demonstrated that first-century Judaism never officially taught a self-achieved works-righteousness in an attempt to earn salvation either. Rather, the Jews recognized that their election and inclusion in the divine covenant was a result of God's merciful choice. First-century Jews believed that it was grace and not unaided human effort that was the cause of their inclusion in the covenant.

Hence, Luther was wrong not only about Catholicism, but also about first-century Palestinian Judaism, to which he compared Catholicism. Once knowledge of these facts reaches popular Christian thinking, advocates of the traditional Protestant doctrine of justification are going to have a difficult time justifying some of their beliefs. The quincentennial anniversary of the Protestant Reformation is liable to coincide with growing popular knowledge of severe cracks in the foundation of Luther's beliefs on justification.

Here is a small sampling of Old Testament Scriptures showing that God's election (choice) of Israel and the divine forgiveness were due to divine mercy and not human merit:

I am not worthy of the least of all the steadfast love and all the faithfulness which thou hast shown to thy servant. (Gen 32:10)

And because he loved your fathers and chose their descendants after them, and brought you out of Egypt with his own presence, by his great power, driving out before you nations greater and mightier than yourselves, to bring you in, to give you their land for an inheritance, as at this day. (Deut 4:37–38)

Be mindful of thy mercy, O Lord, and of thy steadfast
    love, for they have been from of old.
Remember not the sins of my youth, or my transgressions;
    according to thy steadfast love remember me, for thy
    goodness' sake, O Lord! (Ps 25:6–7)

If thou, O Lord, shouldst mark iniquities, Lord, who
    could stand?
But there is forgiveness with thee, that thou mayest be
    feared....
O Israel, hope in the Lord! For with the Lord there is
    steadfast love, and with him is plenteous redemption.
And he will redeem Israel from all his iniquities.
    (Ps 130:3–4, 7–8)

Bless the Lord, O my soul, and forget not all his benefits,
who forgives all your iniquity, who heals all your diseases,
who redeems your life from the Pit, who crowns you with
    steadfast love and mercy....
The Lord is merciful and gracious, slow to anger and
    abounding in steadfast love....
He does not deal with us according to our sins, nor requite
    us according to our iniquities.
For as the heavens are high above the earth, so great is his
    steadfast love toward those who fear him;
as far as the east is from the west, so far does he remove
    our transgressions from us.
As a father pities his children, so the Lord pities those
    who fear him.(Ps 103:2–4, 8, 10–13)

From the sampling of Old Testament verses above, it's apparent that Jews believed in God's gracious mercy for forgiveness. In addition, we'll see in the next section on the historical backdrop to Romans and Galatians, that during the two centuries before Christ, Judaism didn't teach that "works of righteousness" meant earning your own salvation.

So a big question remains, "If first-century Jews didn't believe in works-righteousness to get *into* the covenant, then what was St. Paul so adamant against in Romans and Galatians?" The New Perspective teaches that the works-righteousness that St. Paul strenuously opposed was not that of *obtaining* covenant status, but of *maintaining* it. In other words, the question wasn't how they entered the covenant, but how they maintained their covenantal status. He was primarily concerned with first-century Judaism's erroneous emphasis on *how to stay in* the covenant, not *how to get in*. This is the historical correction to our understanding of the context for St. Paul's discussion on justification and his arguments against "works-righteousness."

In Romans and Galatians, St. Paul is teaching against a specific type of "zeal" found within Judaism that, before his conversion, had deeply motivated him to persecute the Church:

> For you have heard of my former life in *Judaism*, how I persecuted the church of God violently and tried to destroy it; and I advanced in *Judaism* beyond many of my own age among my people, so *extremely zealous* was I for the traditions of my fathers. (Gal 1:13–14; emphasis added)

What was the precise nature of the zeal within first-century Judaism that St. Paul identified with "works-righteousness"? The answer to this question is foundational to building an accurate understanding of St. Paul's teaching on justification. Quoting a few verses from Romans or Galatians to support one's particular view of justification is bound to be distorted if divorced from a historically correct understanding of Judaism's zeal.

The specific zeal motivating Paul before his conversion, as well as those Judaizing teachers troubling the early churches, was a belief in the necessity of works to keep themselves separate from the Gentiles in order to maintain their righteous standing in the covenant. They were seeking justification by their works of separation from the Gentiles. Their chief way of doing this was by maintaining their distinctive Jewish customs, especially circumcision, dietary regulations, and Sabbath-keeping.

Hence the Judaizers' zeal for circumcision that St. Paul opposed in his Epistle to the Galatians was motivated by a desire to maintain Jewish separateness and to oppose Jewish merging with Hellenistic (Greek) culture.

The Historical Backdrop to the Epistles to the Romans and Galatians

The historical events impacting Judaism in the few centuries between Malachi and Matthew, which Protestants call the intertestamental period, are crucial for understanding numerous New Testament passages, especially those pertaining to justification and the relationship between Jews and Gentiles in the early Church.

The Seleucid Empire was a dynasty of thirteen kings that succeeded Alexander the Great (d. 323 B.C.) in the eastern portion of his Macedonian Empire.

To maintain control of this vast territory, the Seleucid kings sought to unify diverse populations by promoting Hellenism. By using Greek culture, language, and customs they hoped to assimilate these populations into a unified empire. Often Hellenization was accomplished by synthesizing Greek culture with local religious, cultural, and philosophical ideas. This strategy met with varying success in parts of the empire, but ran into a stone wall when forced implementation was attempted upon Israel.

Before the rise of the Seleucid Empire, both Judah and Israel experienced fierce divine judgment and foreign captivity because of their moral apostasy, which grew alongside religious syncretism with Canaanite religions. Upon their return from captivity, the Jews, having learned their lesson about religious syncretism, adhered closely to their distinctive Jewish customs, such as circumcision and dietary regulations, to keep themselves faithful to God and separated from Gentiles.

In 169 B.C., the Seleucid ruler, Antiochus IV Epiphanes, took Jerusalem and entered the Holy of Holies, the sacred place reserved for God alone. Seeking to use Hellenistic culture to strengthen his grip over Judea, Antiochus outlawed the religious practices of Judaism. He caused the temple sacrifices to cease and erected a Greek altar to Zeus and established "sacred" prostitution in the temple on December 25, 167 B.C. For these acts, Antiochus is thought of as the forerunner of the Antichrist. His evil acts are in the background of Jesus's statements of the "abomination of desolation" recorded in the Gospels.

Antiochus forbade Sabbath-keeping and circumcision. When it was discovered that two mothers had circumcised their babies, the Hellenists forced the mothers to parade about Jerusalem with their slain babies strung about their necks. After the parade, the mothers were killed by being tossed off the top of the city wall.

Thousands of other Jews who resisted participating in pagan rituals and Hellenistic customs, which included eating food forbidden by Jewish dietary laws, were put to death.

> According to the decree, they put to death the women who had their children circumcised, and their families and those who circumcised them; and they hung the infants from their mothers' necks.

> But many in Israel stood firm and were resolved in their hearts not to eat unclean food. They chose to die rather than to be defiled by food or to profane the holy covenant; and they did die. (1 Macc 1:60–63)

This unspeakably cruel imposition of Hellenism was about to extinguish Judaism. At this dark moment arose Judas ben Maccabees to lead one of the most courageous and inspiring resistance movements in all of human history.

Judas Maccabeus recruitment speech to resist the Hellenization of Antiochus Epiphanies is important for understanding St. Paul's references to "zeal for the law" and to be "reckoned as righteous."

> Now, my children, show zeal for the law, and give your lives for the covenant of our fathers.

> Remember the deeds of the fathers, which they did in their generations; and receive great honor and an everlasting name. Was not *Abraham* found faithful when tested, and it was *reckoned to him as righteousness*? … *Phinehas* our father, because he was *deeply zealous*, received the covenant of everlasting priesthood." (1 Macc 2:50–52, 54; emphasis added)

Zeal for the law in this context is specific, namely, resistance to Hellenism. Note that Abraham and Phinehas are both mentioned in a passage highlighting the ancient fathers who were zealous for the law. It is significant that the only two people specifically mentioned as "reckoned as righteous" in the entire Old Testament were Abraham and Phinehas.

A key passage in St. Paul relating to justification is Romans 4:3: "For what does the scripture say? 'Abraham believed God, and it was reckoned to him as righteousness.'" In this passage, Paul shows that Abraham was "reckoned as righteous" because of his faith (i.e., justified by faith).

What act did Phinehas perform so that he was "reckoned as righteousness"? In an episode early in Israel's history, the redeemed nation was seduced into pagan idolatry and immorality by the advice of Balaam. Israel ignored its separation from Gentile paganism and yoked itself to Baal. In defiant rebellion to the law, an Israelite man brought a pagan woman into his tent in the sight of all Israel. Phinehas, jealous for God and zealous for the law, took a spear and struck it through both the man and the woman pinning them to the ground (Num 25:6–13). For this bold act of keeping Israel separate from pagan Gentiles, Phinehas was reckoned as righteous. "Then Phinehas stood up and interposed, / and the plague was stayed. / And that has been *reckoned to him as righteousness* / from generation to generation for ever" (Ps 106:30–31; emphasis added).

Centuries later, Judas Maccabeus used the example of Phinehas to rally the Israelites to resist the forced Hellenism of Antiochus. Against impossible odds, the Maccabean revolt was successful. In 165 B.C., Judas Maccabeus marched victoriously into Jerusalem. Hellenism was expelled, the temple cleansed, and the proper worship of God was restored. The Feast of Hanukkah (Dedication) was established to commemorate the cleansing and rededication of the temple. As a faithful Jew, Jesus himself attended the Feast of Hanukkah in Jerusalem (Jn 10:22).

Arising from the lessons learned from the Babylonian captivity and from the life-and-death struggle ensuing from the imposition of Hellenism by Antiochus, a pious Jew was fiercely zealous for the law by maintaining the distance between Judaism and the corrupting influences of Hellenism.

The Pharisees (literally "separated ones") we read about in the New Testament arose following the Maccabean revolt. They were initially part of a group known as the Hasideans, the "loyal ones" who were zealous for maintaining the traditions of the law. This movement split into two groups. The Pharisees became the majority group centered in Jerusalem. The minority groups, like the Qumran community, seeking even more rigid separation from public life, withdrew to the deserted areas east of Jerusalem.

Before his conversion, Paul was a dedicated Pharisee. In his self-description, he says that he was "extremely zealous" for Jewish traditions. "I advanced in Judaism beyond many of my own age among my people, so *extremely zealous* was I for the traditions of my fathers" (Gal 1:14; emphasis added).

Paul's zeal needs be understood in the historical context of the Pharisaical movement. Paul was a premier first-century version of Phinehas and a Judas Maccabeus—an honorable Jew sensing that his solemn duty was to protect the wall between Jew and Gentile. When he saw the early Church mingling Jews and Gentiles without circumcision and dietary laws (i.e., "the works of the law), he was filled with rage. Paul's anti-Hellenist zeal was the motivating force behind his fierce persecution of the early Church.

> Though I myself have reason for confidence in the flesh
> also. If any other man thinks he has reason for confidence
> in the flesh, I have more: circumcised on the eighth day,
> of the people of Israel, of the tribe of Benjamin, a Hebrew
> born of Hebrews; as to the law a *Pharisee*, as to *zeal* a
> persecutor of the church, as to *righteousness under the
> law* blameless. (Phil 3:4–6; emphasis added)

Little known to Paul before his conversion, he was divinely chosen before birth to be the key person at a decisive moment in salvation history to tear down the wall separating Jew and Gentile. The chief proponent of separation between Jew and Gentile was knocked off his horse, and his life course was literally changed 180 degrees. St. Paul was now the chosen instrument to make known to the world that in the New Covenant the promises to Abraham were open to both Jew and Gentile.

With this historical background in mind, we can gain fresh insight into many New Testament passages.

In Acts, St. Stephen was chosen for the diaconate when "the disciples were increasing in number" and "the Hellenists murmured against the Hebrews" for being neglected. As he reached out to Gentile Christians, Stephen was charged with changing the customs of Moses, saying that they didn't apply to the Gentiles. It's no coincidence that Paul supported those stoning the forerunner of the early Church's mission to the Hellenists.

The first Church council, in Acts 15, dealt with the question of whether or not the Gentile converts needed to maintain the "customs of Moses," especially circumcision. The council decided that Gentile converts to Christianity did not need to maintain the distinguishing marks of Judaism.

In Galatians 2, Paul recounts how he firmly resisted Peter for his refusal to eat with Gentile converts. Also in Galatians, chapter 3, are some of Paul's strongest words directed against those seeking to require circumcision for Gentile converts. Paul taught that since God had removed the wall between Jew and Gentile, there was no longer a need for the works of the law (i.e., the separation practices of dietary regulations and circumcision).

The Epistle to the Romans

The relationship between Jewish and Gentile Christians pervades every major section in the Epistle to the Romans.

The historian Suetonius records that in A.D. 49, the Emperor Claudius expelled all Jews from Rome. It seems there was intense rioting over the introduction of Christianity in Rome. The many Jewish converts in the Church were among the larger group of Jews forced to leave Rome.

In Acts 18:1–3, we read that two Jewish Christians, Aquila and Priscilla, came and joined St. Paul in Corinth, Greece, after being expelled with the other Jews from Rome. Around A.D. 56–57, St. Paul wrote the Epistle to the Romans from Corinth toward the completion of his third missionary journey (Rom 15:23ff. and Acts 20:1–3). By that time, Aquila and Priscilla were back in Rome (Rom 16:3).

The reintroduction of these Jewish Christians into a now Gentile-dominated church caused immense tensions that the Epistle to the Romans was written to calm. St. Paul also had Gentile mission plans for Europe and therefore needed a unified church at Rome for a base of operations.

Jew and Gentile Theme

Throughout the Epistle to the Romans runs a Jew-and-Gentile theme:

- In establishing the theme of the Epistle (1:16–17), St. Paul says that the Gospel is for both Jew and Gentile.

- Romans 1:18–3:20: "Both Jews and Greeks are under the power of sin."

- Romans 3:21: Both Jew and Gentile are saved (justified) by faith—the common way of salvation.

- Chapter 4: Abraham is the father of both the circumcised and uncircumcised.

- Chapter 5: Christ, the new Adam, is the source of life for the entire community of the redeemed.

- Chapter 6: Baptism unites all believers (Jew and Gentile) in Christ. All (Jew and Gentile) who were slaves to sin now have a new source of obedience to God.

- Chapter 8: Both Jew and Gentile have the Spirit of sonship. Therefore, both are the adopted children of God.

- Chapters 9–11: Jew and Gentile in redemptive history

- Romans 12–15a: practical exhortations to Jewish and Gentile Christians for living in harmony within the Church, not to squabble over dietary differences among believers

- Romans 15b: mission plans to Gentile lands and charitable support for Jewish Christians in Jerusalem

The Epistle to the Romans teaches that both Jew and Gentile have the following: the common problem of sin (chaps. 1–3), a common path to salvation in justification by faith (chaps. 3–4), a common spiritual father in Abraham (chap. 4), a common Savior (chap. 5), a common sharing of life in the new covenant (chaps. 5–8), a common indwelling of the Spirit of sonship (chap. 8), a common plan of salvation (chaps. 9–11), and a common life in the Church (chaps. 12–15).

In a nutshell, St. Paul's emphasis in Romans and Galatians wasn't a strike against Pelagianism (earn-it-yourself salvation), since this wasn't the chief problem with Judaism's influence in the early Church. Rather, the central problem was Jewish Christians trying to force Gentile Christians to practice "works-righteousness," that is, keeping Jewish food laws, practicing circumcision, and keeping the Sabbath and other Jewish festivals. St. Paul insists that for both Jew and Gentile, justification (i.e., righteousness) is attained by faith and Spirit-empowered obedience—and not by these distinctively Jewish practices.

The standard Protestant charge of "work righteousness" against Catholics should have evaporated with the Council of Trent's teaching on justification. Trent was a repetition of the timeless teaching of the Catholic Church that one can never merit salvation by his own effort. This unbroken chain of teaching continues in the *Catechism of the Catholic Church* with the assertion that, "Our justification comes from the grace of God."[2] Unfortunately, most Protestants only hear carefully extracted and out-of-context portions of Trent, strung together to convey the impression that Catholics believe in a "do-it yourself" salvation. Amazingly, this tactic has worked successfully for five centuries, convincing most Protestants that Catholics are little more than modern-day Judaistic practitioners, striving to earn their own salvation.

The New Perspective fundamentally alters the classical debate between Protestants and Catholics by showing that Catholics have been unfairly compared to a theological ghost—a conception of first-century Judaism which lacks historical existence. Once Protestants discover the historical inaccuracies regarding first-century Judaism's approach to salvation, I hope they will take a closer look at Catholicism, which is so often compared to this false picture of Judaism.

The history of the early Church and the history of first-century Judaism studied through primary documents are close friends of Catholicism. My expectation is that the Catholic Church will have new friends when a more accurate history of first-century Judaism becomes more widely known.

Synthesis View of the Traditional and New Perspectives

Currently, most New Testament scholars are lining up either for or against the New Perspective. As both perspectives challenge each other, a refinement process will produce modifications to each perspective. There are notable attempts to develop a synthesis from both views.[3] It is true that new scholarly insights have a tendency to overstate and overdevelop a new position and to discard a bit too much of the previous views. Yet, a complementary view still must have a dominant viewpoint if one of the two perspectives leads to a more precise interpretation of St. Paul's Epistles by using the most historically accurate religious and cultural context to his writings. The dominant viewpoint is going to be the New Perspective since it is more accurately based on the historical record of first-century Judaism.

Man-on-the-Street Pelagianism

First-century Judaism officially taught that salvation is by God's grace and mercy. Was it then one-hundred-percent immune from beliefs in salvation by self-achieved legalistic efforts? Probably it was not, if modern ill-formed religious tendencies to trust in oneself for salvation are in any way similar to those in the first-century.

Today, despite the official teaching of both Protestant churches and the Catholic Church, millions of professing Christians when asked about what basis they hope to gain entrance into heaven say, "I've tried to be a good person." Evangelical Protestants do a much better job than mainline Protestants and Catholics at teaching their people the need for a fundamental dependence on the grace of God, rather than themselves. Yet, there are significant segments in each group (Evangelical Protestants, mainline Protestants, and Catholics) who fail to grasp the fundamental teaching on salvation by their churches.

First-century Judaism could easily have experienced this same disconnect between official teaching and man-on-the-street beliefs that we see in our day. Every generation seems to struggle with the recurring impulse toward self-achieved salvation. Therefore, the continuing need to hear St. Paul's message emphasizing that salvation is by the grace of God—without the false portrayals of Catholic beliefs and first-century Judaism.

Chapter Twelve

Justification and Divinization by Grace

Just how great is the greatness of God's grace in justification? St. Augustine said that "the justification of the wicked is a greater work than the creation of heaven and earth."[1]

Eight centuries later, St. Thomas Aquinas, discussing the effects of grace, reaffirmed the teaching of Augustine and boldly stated, "The good of grace in one is greater than the good of nature in the whole universe."[2] Is there something Sts. Augustine and Aquinas knew about the greatness of justification that many of us have neglected, or never known?

Many of you may find the contents of this chapter shocking. I was sorely tempted to skip over this topic, fearing that it might seem beyond the boundaries of belief. Yet, I've promised to demonstrate the surpassing greatness of grace in the Catholic doctrine of justification, and this is where it reaches its pinnacle. So, let's dig in.

As we launch into this topic, let me remind you that Catholic beliefs on justification involve a constellation of God's works of grace, including the remission of sins, Baptism, adoption, infusion of God's sanctifying grace resulting in interior sanctification, the gift of the Holy Spirit—the spirit of sonship. Cardinal Newman aptly expressed the Catholic view by saying, "The doctrine of justifying faith is a summary of the whole process of salvation from first to last."[3]

Protestants believe in the works of grace mentioned above, but assert that they are separate and subsequent to justification in the order of salvation. To put it simply, Protestants insist that justification is limited to an external work of grace, a legal declaration of "not guilty," thus resulting in the forgiveness of sins. Catholics also believe that justification results in the remission of sins, but unlike Protestants, Catholics go much further, believing that justification also involves the "sanctification and renewal of the inner man."[4]

As we've previously discussed, a careful reading of the relevant sections of the canons and decrees of the Council of Trent and the *Catechism of the Catholic Church* reveal that adoption is a valuable key for unlocking the heart of justification.[5] Therefore, in order to penetrate the excellence of God's grace we have to ask, "What is the nature and extent of God's grace in justification and adoption?" The profound discovery of one's identity in relation to God the Father, the Son, and the Holy Spirit is life-changing.

The *Catechism of the Catholic Church* in the section titled "Grace and Justification," clearly answers the extent of God's grace in the Catholic view of justification and adoption in four important paragraphs.

> Our justification comes from the grace of God. Grace is favor, the free and undeserved help that God gives us to respond to his call to become children of God, adoptive sons, partakers of the divine nature and of eternal life.

Grace is a participation in the life of God. It introduces us into the intimacy of Trinitarian life: by Baptism the Christian participates in the grace of Christ, the Head of his Body. As an "adopted son" he can henceforth call God "Father," in union with the only Son. He receives the life of the Spirit who breathes charity into him and who forms the Church.

The grace of Christ is the gratuitous gift that God makes to us of his own life, infused by the Holy Spirit into our soul to heal it of sin and to sanctify it. It is the sanctifying or deifying grace received in Baptism. It is in us the source of the work of sanctification: "Therefore if any one is in Christ, he is a new creation; the old has passed away, behold, the new has come. All this is from God, who through Christ reconciled us to himself."

Through the power of the Holy Spirit we take part in Christ's Passion by dying to sin, and in his Resurrection by being born to a new life; we are members of his Body which is the Church, branches grafted onto the vine which is himself: "[God] gave himself to us through his Spirit. By the participation of the Spirit, we become communicants in the divine nature. . . . For this reason, those in whom the Spirit dwells are divinized."[6]

You might be asking yourself, "What is this strange talk about deifying grace, partaking of the divine nature, and becoming divinized?" This sounds like something coming from a guest on *The Oprah Winfrey Show.* It also sounds like the declarations of the New Age gurus who say that one's inner self is really a god since we are all part of the great oneness of the universe. Yes, Catholic beliefs on deification may sound similar, but remember that every deadly counterfeit notion has teachings that mimic the truth enough to deceive. There are categorical differences between New Age beliefs and Catholic ones.

It is necessary to begin an investigation into divinization by stating what it doesn't mean. Becoming deified or divinized doesn't indicate that we share in the *essence* of God in any manner. The deified person never stops being a finite human creature. We don't ever become God, or a part of God. The divinized person is not absorbed into the deity in a manner that he ceases being a human person. Divinization does not occur as a result of self-achievement, self-realization, or self-actualization.

After considering what deification isn't, let's look at what deification is. *Deification* is a term referring to the utterly profound transformation of human nature by divine grace into the likeness of the Son of God. Stemming from justification and adoption is a real covenant union with Christ that's an actual sharing in Trinitarian life, resulting in what is synonymously termed divinization, deification, theosis, or participation in God.

Deification (or divinization) refers to that aspect of our union with Christ in which we share in Jesus's unique sonship with the Father as adopted sons and daughters. This sharing in sonship should add a *much* deeper appreciation of what it means to be "in Christ." Jesus prayed,

> that they may all be one; even as thou, Father, art in me, and I in thee, that they also may be in us ... The glory which thou hast given me I have given to them, that they may be one even as we are one, I in them and thou in me ...that the world may know that thou hast sent me and hast loved them even as thou hast loved me. (Jn 17:21–23)

Protestant theologian Clark Pinnock highlights the sonship aspect of divinization when he says:

> Through Son and Spirit, God is leading humanity to union with himself. He wants us to share the Son's filial relationship with himself.

> By taking on our nature and becoming human, Jesus raised humanity to the level of the Son in relation to the Father.... As a result, we all in union with Christ by the power of the Spirit are enabled to participate in divine life.

> Salvation, then, is more than relief at not being condemned: it sweeps us up into the love of God for participation in the divine nature.[7]

I repeat, as we are deified we don't cease being human. Rather, the process of divinization is to become more and more of what it truly means to reach the fullness of human personhood in the image and likeness of God. St. Paul described the transformative divinization process in 2 Corinthians: "We all, with unveiled face, beholding the glory of the LORD, are being changed into his likeness from one degree of glory to another; for this comes from the Lord who is the Spirit" (3:18).

There is an inward glorification/divinization process in the present age (2 Cor 3:17–18 and 4:6–7, 16–17).[8] The final phase of deification is at the end of this age where, upon Christ's return, we receive glorified (i.e., divinized) human bodies as we enter our full inheritance as adopted sons and daughters (Rom 8:18–24). At the same time as we receive our glorified bodies, the entire cosmos is divinized, or glorified, The new heavens and new earth will have no need of a sun since the glory of the Lord will be its dazzling light (Rev 21:23–24).

Three Scriptures on Justification and Divinization

Three Scripture passages cited in the footnotes of the *Catechism*'s section on justification and divinization are worthy of investigation. The passages are 2 Peter 1:3–4; John 1:12–14, 16; and Romans 8:14–17. I'll comment on each of these three passages in the order mentioned.

2 Peter 1:3–4

Notice carefully in the passage below from 2 Peter that it says that God has "called us to his own glory and excellence" based upon his "precious and very great promises." Next St. Peter makes the explicit declaration that this calling entails becoming "partakers of the divine nature."

> His divine power has granted to us all things that pertain to life and godliness, through the knowledge of him who called us to his own glory and excellence, by which he has granted to us his precious and very great promises, that through these you may escape from the corruption that is in the world because of passion, and become partakers of the divine nature. (2 Pet 1:3–4)

Have you heard many sermons on the incredible truth in 2 Peter 1:3–4? Even though I preached hundreds of sermons and taught countless Bible studies while a Protestant minister, I can't remember ever commenting on this passage. How many of us have ever stopped long enough during our devotional reading of Scripture to ponder the depth of this "precious and very great promise?" In the past, I read over it without much of a pause. Now, I read this verse and have to stop and shake my head in astonishment at the extent of God's grace in our salvation.

John 1:12–14, 16

The second passage cited by the *Catechism* in the sections discussing grace, justification, adoption, and divinization is from the first chapter of the Gospel according to St. John:

> But to all who received him, who believed in his name, he gave power to become children of God; who were born, not of blood nor of the will of the flesh nor of the will of man, but of God.

> And the Word became flesh and dwelt among us, full of grace and truth; we have beheld his glory, glory as of the only Son from the Father…. And from his fulness have we all received, grace upon grace. (Jn 1:12–14, 16)

You might ask, "What does a Scripture passage talking about the Incarnation have to do with divinization?" The short answer is "Everything!" It is because God became man that man can become divinized. Scott Hahn succinctly describes the relationship between the Incarnation and deification saying, Jesus humanized his divinity, but he also divinized humanity."[9] St. John says that Jesus was filled with his Father's glory. Then from the fullness of the Son of God who became man, we receive "grace upon grace," that is, grace to an unimaginable degree.

When discussing the Incarnation, the *Catechism* states, "The Word became flesh to make us *'partakers of the divine nature.'*"[10]

St. Irenaeus, the second-century defender of the Faith, in his classic work *Against Heresies* said: "For this is why the Word became man, and the Son of God became the Son of man: so that man, by entering into communion with the Word and thus receiving divine sonship, might become a son of God."[11]

St. Athanasius, in his famous work *On the Incarnation*, succinctly states the unfathomable connection between the Incarnation and deification: "For the Son of God became man so that we might become God."[12]

These words are jarring to many modern Christians' ears, but remember that they come from St. Athanasius, the heroic fourth-century defender of Jesus's deity against the Arian heresy and a man recognized as a Doctor of the Church by both the Orthodox and Catholics. Rest assured, St. Athanasius isn't advocating that we become a part of the essence of God, but he is boldly setting forth a goal of salvation that far exceeds simply having sins remitted.

St. Augustine is claimed as one of the foremost Church Fathers in the theological lineage of Lutherans, Presbyterians, the Reformed, and many other Protestants. Unfortunately, they don't follow St. Augustine when he explicitly connects justification, adoption, and deification as unified aspects of God's redeeming grace ultimately stemming from the Incarnation:

> It is evident then, that He hath called men gods, that are deified of His Grace, not born of His Substance. For He doth justify, who is just through His own self ... But He that justifieth doth Himself deify, in that by justifying He doth makes son of God. "For He hath given them power to become the sons of God" (John 1:12).[13]

> If we have been made sons of God, we have also been made gods: but this is the effect of Grace adopting, not of nature generating. For the only Son of God ... with the Father, Our Lord and Savior Jesus Christ, was in the beginning the Word, and the Word with God, the Word God. The rest that are made gods, are made by His own Grace, are not born of His Substance, that they should be

the same as He, but by favor they should come to Him, and be fellow-heirs with Christ.[14]

For if He who is by nature the Son of God was made the Son of man through mercy for the sake of the sons of men … how much more credible is it that the sons of men by nature should be made the sons of God by the grace of God, and should dwell in God, in whom alone and from whom alone the blessed can be made partakers of that immortality?[15]

Before casually dismissing deification as a crazy notion, consider the consistent testimonies of Sts. Irenaeus, Athanasius, and Augustine cited above. Yes, their statements are startling, but astonishment is the proper reaction to God's plan of salvation. Rather than closing our minds to deification, we need to pray for the opening of our eyes to the magnitude of God's grace.

Romans 8:14–17

The third Scripture passage the *Catechism* cites in support of grace, justification, adoption, and deification is Romans 8:14–17.

For all who are led by the Spirit of God are sons of God. For you did not receive the spirit of slavery to fall back into fear, but you have received the spirit of sonship. When we cry, "Abba! Father!" it is the Spirit himself bearing witness with our spirit that we are children of God, and if children, then heirs, heirs of God and fellow heirs with Christ, provided we suffer with him in order that we may also be glorified with him.

This passage highlights that it is through the power of the indwelling Holy Spirit that our communion with Trinitarian life is established. This covenant union as adopted sons and daughters is a real participation in the life of God and the partaking of the

121

divine nature. Hence, as the result of the grace of justification, we can truly call the Almighty and Everlasting God, "Abba! Father!"

Ancient and Modern Teaching on Deification

St. Athanasius, the courageous defender of Christian orthodoxy mentioned above, said the following about the Holy Spirit's role in divinization: "[God] gave himself to us through his Spirit. By the participation of the Spirit, we become communicants in the divine nature. . . . For this reason, those in whom the Spirit dwells are divinized."[16]

Descriptions of divinization by the Church Fathers were never intended to imply that men become a part of the essence of God, yet they are intended to elevate our thoughts about the degree of grace that profoundly transforms us and allows us to share in the life of the Trinity. The language of divinization seems shocking to most modern ears, except for Eastern Catholics and those in the Orthodox churches, where the timeless teaching of deification hasn't faded from the memory of Christians.

Pope St. John Paul II described the Eastern Christian's goal of salvation as follows:

> And so, made "sharers of the divine nature" (2 Pet 1:4) they enter into communion with the most holy Trinity. These features describe the Eastern outlook of the Christian. His or her goal is participation in the divine nature through communion with the mystery of the Holy Trinity.
>
> Participation in Trinitarian life takes place through the liturgy and in a special way through the Eucharist, the mystery of communion with the glorified body of Christ, the seed of immortality. In divinization and particularly

in the sacraments, Eastern theology attributes a very special role to the Holy Spirit: through the power of the Spirit who dwells in man deification already begins on earth; the creature is transfigured and God's kingdom inaugurated.[17]

I realize that many Protestant Charismatics and Pentecostals are sincere Christians who left the Catholic Church and her sacraments in search of a greater experience of the Holy Spirit. As one who has lived and ministered in Pentecostal and Charismatic circles, I urge those seeking the ultimate fullness of the Spirit to consider what the *Catechism* has to say about the Spirit, the sacraments, and divinization.

> The Father always hears the prayer of his Son's Church which, in the epiclesis [the prayer by which the priest invokes the Holy Spirit] of each sacrament, expresses her faith in the power of the Spirit. As fire transforms into itself everything it touches, so the Holy Spirit transforms into the divine life whatever is subjected to his power. [18]

You might be surprised to learn that John Calvin alluded to deification, although he never used the term. Calvin certainly wouldn't unite the concepts of justification, adoption, and deification as Catholics and Orthodox would, yet he did mention the process of deification in his commentary on 2 Peter:

> The greatness of his grace cannot be sufficiently conceived by our minds. Therefore this consideration alone ought to be abundantly sufficient to make us to renounce the world and to carry us aloft to heaven. Let us then mark, that the end of the gospel is, to render us eventually conformable to God, and, if we may so speak, to deify us.[19]

Protestant scholar, Clark H. Pinnock, carefully distinguishes divinization from pantheism, then highlights the believer's participation in Trinitarian life, and finally asserts that justification involves more than what is commonly understood by his fellow Protestants.

What we call union (theosis or divinization) is not pantheism—there is no absorption of the person in God. By the grace of God and as creatures we participate in him.

Union with God begins on earth and is not reserved entirely for the future. Believers, in Christ by the Spirit, are beginning to participate in God and experience the love pouring from the Father to the Son.

In justifying sinners God is not engaging in fantasies, but declaring that they have been incorporated into the victory of Jesus Christ. Salvation, then, is more than relief at not being condemned; it sweeps us up into the love of God for participation in the divine nature. The key thing is that salvation involves transformation. It is not cheap grace, based on bare assent to propositions, or merely a change of status.[20]

Adoption isn't just an abstract theological doctrine, and being called a child of God isn't just a name without a corresponding reality. As a result of justification and adoption, God shares his very life with us and in us. The result is that God's children are transformed into his image.

St. Paul says, "For those whom he foreknew he also predestined to be *conformed* to the image of his Son, in order that he might be the first-born among many brethren" (Rom 8:29; my italics). The Greek word (*symmorphous*) translated as "conformed" here means "to take the same form," denoting an "inward and thorough and not merely superficial likeness."[21]

In Romans 12:2, St. Paul says, "Do not be conformed to this

world but be transformed [Gk. *metamorphous*] by the renewal of your mind." Here St. Paul urges a metamorphosis, that is, a mega-transformation by supernatural means. The sharing in Trinitarian life is what brings about this transformation.

God's eternal purpose for his children is that they become conformed into the image of his Son (Rom 8:29). This transformation takes place in this life as an internal metamorphosis (Rom 12:2) and culminates in the glorious resurrection of the just on the last day (Rom 8:18–19, 23).

What I Missed in Mere Christianity

It shouldn't be a surprise that C. S. Lewis, a lover of old books and a student of Athanasius, mentions the process of deification in *Mere Christianity*. Yet for years I missed the full implications of deification in the concluding pages of one of my favorite Christian books. Lewis writes:

> The command *Be ye perfect* is not idealistic gas. Nor is it a command to do the impossible. He is going to make us into creatures that can obey that command. He said (in the Bible) that we were "gods" and He is going to make good on His words…. He will make the feeblest and filthiest of us into a god or goddess, dazzling, radiant, immortal creature, pulsating all through with such energy and joy and wisdom and love as we cannot now imagine….
>
> God became man to turn creatures into sons; not simply to produce better men of the old kind but to produce a new kind of man….
>
> The next step has already appeared … it is a change that goes off in a totally different direction—a change from being creatures of God to being sons of God….

For now the critical moment has arrived. Century by century God has guided nature up to the point of producing creatures which can (if they will) be taken right out of nature, turned into "gods.".…

The new step has been taken and is being taken. Already the new men are dotted here and there all over the earth.[22]

Catholic beliefs on justification open to us vistas of a Father who certainly forgives, but also loves his undeserving children to the degree of elevating them to a life-transforming union with Himself. Historic Christian beliefs on justification never limited God's grace in justification to something resembling a judge making a "not-guilty" pronouncement.

If there is a "fault" with Catholicism's beliefs on justification it is that they proclaim too much grace. There is no rational explanation for God outpouring such a rich and comprehensive measure of grace upon his children. There is absolutely none. Yet believing in immeasurable grace isn't a fault—it's the essence of the Good News.

The real question with justification between Protestants and Catholics is over the extent of grace. I ask you, my Evangelical friends: Should a sixteenth-century definition of justification be allowed to limit the enormity of God's grace in what the heavenly Father does in the lives of his sons and daughters?

If we are on the right track in understanding God's grace, the proper view should be one that is so expansive that we need a gift of grace even to begin to comprehend it. St. Paul said that realization of the plan of grace is best grasped on one's knees:

For this reason I bow my knees before the Father, from whom every family in heaven and on earth is named, that according to the riches of his glory he may grant you to be strengthened with might through his Spirit in the inner man, and that Christ may dwell in your hearts through faith; that you, being rooted and grounded in love, may have power to comprehend with all the saints what is the breadth and length and height and depth, and to know the love of Christ which surpasses knowledge, that you may be filled with all the fulness of God.

Now to him who by the power at work within us is able to do far more abundantly than all that we ask or think, to him be glory in the church and in Christ Jesus to all generations, for ever and ever. Amen. (Eph 3:14–21)

The Weight of Glory

What should we visualize when we sing in "Amazing Grace" the stanza beginning, "When we've been there ten thousand years bright shining as the sun"? C. S. Lewis in *The Weight of Glory* amusingly pops many distorted mental conceptions of glorification by asking, "Who wishes to become a kind of living electric light bulb?"[23]

Thankfully, grace doesn't make us into electric light bulbs. The glory that God radiates through us is not an abstract and person-less energy, like the power that flows through power utility lines. Rather the glorious luminance that shines through us is not a thing, but a person: the Light of the World who is full of grace and full of glory.

Lewis affirms a little further on in *The Weight of Glory* that everyone's deepest desire is be loved by God as a father delights in a son with "a weight of glory which our thoughts can hardly sustain."[24] Everyone's deepest desire can be fulfilled by prayerfully appropriating the Catholic teaching on amazing grace, justification, adoption, and divinization.

> For it is the God who said, "Let light shine out of darkness," who has shone in our hearts to give the light of the knowledge of the glory of God in the face of Christ.

> But we have this treasure in earthen vessels, to show that the transcendent power belongs to God and not to us....

> ...So we do not lose heart. Though our outer nature is wasting away, our inner nature is being renewed every day. For this slight momentary affliction is preparing for us an eternal weight of glory beyond all comparison. (2 Cor 4:6–7, 16–17)

Ecumenical Documents on Justification

As mentioned above in chapter 2, recent ecumenical documents on justification are probably not the best way for nonexperts to discover what the Catholic Church teaches about justification. These are technical documents written by expert theologians who already understand both perspectives. Several misinterpretations of the justification ecumenical documents have been widely spread by religious media.

This does not mean that I perceive the ecumenical movement's attempts to bridge divisions on justification as unimportant. On the contrary, I agree with the opening statement of Vatican II's Decree on Ecumenism, which said, "The restoration of unity among all Christians is one of the principal concerns of the Second Vatican Council. Christ the Lord founded one Church and one Church only.... Division openly contradicts the will of Christ, scandalizes the world, and damages the holy cause of preaching the Gospel to every creature."[1]

Therefore, my criticisms of the ecumenical documents highlighted below are not censures against the noble efforts to gain Catholic and Evangelical unity, but rather cautions directed primarily toward their use by non-theologians.

"The Gift of Salvation"

Two major ecumenical statements relating to justification were issued during the late 1990s. The first was the document published in 1997, "The Gift of Salvation," produced by an unofficial group of prominent Evangelical laymen and Catholic spokesmen.[2] The document, signed by both Evangelical and Catholic representatives, made the striking statement: "We understand that what we here affirm is in agreement with what the reformation traditions have meant by justification by faith alone (*sola fide*)."

I have tracked articles since the issuance of this document and can attest that widespread confusion, division, and discord have erupted within Evangelical circles. Evangelical Protestant theologian Dr. John H. Armstrong said the document was "an affirmation of unity which accepts the actual slogans of the Reformation without agreeing on the actual content of the slogans."[3]

Evangelical opposition to "The Gift of Salvation" prompted the formation of the Alliance of Confessing Evangelicals (ACE) under the chairmanship of Dr. James Boice (now deceased). The organization included Evangelical scholars, authors, and pastors, including R.C. Sproul, John Armstrong, and Michael Horton. The new organization claims that "The Gift of Salvation" caused deep divisions among Evangelicals.

The Religion and Society Report said that "The Gift of Salvation" was causing "ecumenical indigestion" instead of hoped-for unity.[4] My caution to anyone trying to use "The Gift of Salvation" to bridge the differences between Catholics and Evangelicals is that you may end up in the middle of a bitter Evangelical dispute.

The flagship Evangelical magazine, *Christianity Today,* reported: "Among the concerns critics have expressed is that public statements do not accurately represent the Catholic church. According to this argument, the evangelical public might be wrongly led to believe the Catholic church has conformed to a Reformational position on justification when, in fact, the only ones who have changed are the handful of people who signed these documents."[5]

Drs. Timothy George, Thomas C. Oden, and J. I. Packer, all distinguished Evangelical scholars, issued "An Open Letter in an attempt to heal the Evangelical division over 'The Gift of Salvation.'" In their letter, they stated, "Our methodology in crafting 'The Gift of Salvation' was to study the Bible together and to formulate a statement on salvation derived from and based upon the evidence of Holy Scripture alone." This letter didn't succeed in healing the divisions within Evangelicalism created by "The Gift of Salvation."

In addition, the "Open Letter" reopened a prime question many Catholics have about Protestant beliefs on justification, namely, "Where does it say in the Bible that justification is by faith *alone*? Isn't the only instance in Holy Scripture when 'justification by faith *alone*' is mentioned James 2:24, where it is negated?" It is confusing to read that the central finding claims to be "based upon the evidence of Holy Scripture alone" when Scripture explicitly refutes the concept.

Joint Declaration on the Doctrine of Justification: Lutheran World Federation and the Catholic Church

The second major ecumenical document relating to justification is "The Joint Declaration on the Doctrine of Justification" signed on October 31, 1999, the 482nd anniversary of the Protestant Reformation, in Augsburg, Germany. This document is an official agreement sign by representatives of the Catholic Church and the Lutheran World Federation.

The "Joint Declaration," like the unofficial "Gift of Salvation" document, appeared to embrace essential Protestant positions on justification in the main text of the document. Yet the Catholic Church saw the need to issue an important annexed statement with several elucidations and clarifications underlying the consensus statements. Church officials didn't want erroneous interpretations to stem from the joint declaration. When reading the declaration, it is necessary to read carefully and understand the concerns underlying the annexed statements. Otherwise, you'll end up with distorted thoughts about current Catholic views on justification.

After the signing of the 1999 "Joint Declaration," many secular media outlets reported that much of the Evangelical community thought the Reformation was over and Luther won the argument. It appeared that Catholics officially and finally admitted Luther's doctrine of justification was the correct one.

Cardinal Edward Cassidy, the President of the Pontifical Council for Promoting Christian Unity, was the lead Catholic negotiator in the formation of the "Joint Declaration." When Cardinal Cassidy was asked by a reporter if there was anything in the declaration that was contrary to the [Catholic] Council of Trent, he replied: "Absolutely not, otherwise how could we do it? We cannot do something contrary to an ecumenical council. There's nothing there that the Council of Trent condemns."[6] Anyone trying to accurately interpret the Catholic view of this document should keep Cardinal Cassidy's statement in mind.

The Lutherans signing this document represent liberal-leaning mainline Protestants. Some of the Lutheran groups signing the "Joint Declaration" are open to abortion, women's ordination, and homosexuality. The usefulness of this document is mainly with liberal mainline Lutherans. Conservative Lutherans, like the Lutheran Church–Missouri Synod and the Wisconsin Evangelical Lutheran Synod, adamantly rejected it as a betrayal of the Gospel. Therefore, the Joint Declaration does not speak for the entire world Lutheranism. In addition, the document doesn't speak for thousands of other non-Lutheran Protestant groups. This document may have helped ecumenical relations with modernist mainline Protestants, but it has generated confusion and division among most Evangelical Protestants.

I have found most Evangelicals delighted to center a discussion on justification by carefully defining each other's beliefs, and then presenting the Biblical and historical basis for those respective beliefs. In my experience, clarity and theological precision will make ecumenical headway. Although complete agreement with the Catholic perspective usually isn't immediately forthcoming, a wholesome ecumenical respect does emerge once Catholic beliefs and their origin in Scripture and Church history are accurately understood.

My desire is to see Evangelicals and Catholics get together and discover unity. The best path for most Evangelicals starts with a firsthand investigation of Catholicism, using the understandable and authoritative resources mentioned in chapter 2, especially the *Catechism of the Catholic Church*. You then compare these Catholic beliefs with Scripture.

The ultimate step in getting Evangelicals and Catholics together is for Evangelicals to reunify with the One, Holy, Catholic, and Apostolic Church—the one Jesus founded.

As an Evangelical convert to Catholicism, charity demands that I share nothing less with you. Otherwise, I would be short-changing my Evangelical friends by suggesting they settle for a written agreement instead.

Appendix II

Sola Gratia, Solo Christo:

The Roman Catholic Doctrine of Justification
Essay by Richard A. White
Submitted to Dr. Harold O.J. Brown
Trinity Evangelical Divinity School

Introduction

The doctrine of justification was, as John Calvin stated, the "hinge of the reformation." James Buchanan provides us with the classic "reformed" definition: "Justification is a legal, or forensic, term, and is used in Scripture to denote the acceptance of any one as righteous in the sight of God."[1] Understood in this way, justification is purely extrinsic to the sinner, inasmuch as he is justified solely on the basis of Christ's righteousness graciously imputed to him. The sinner does not become righteous himself, but because he trusts in Christ's work for him, he is considered innocent by God the judge. In this way, works contribute nothing to justification; it is by faith alone.

In contrast is the Roman Catholic position, which sadly, few evangelicals even bother to consider, let alone understand. In many cases, the issue is naively boiled down to justification by faith, on the one hand (evangelicalism), versus justification by works, on the other hand (Roman Catholicism). This crass caricature has little basis in reality, and hampers the cause for theological truth and Christian unity. In this essay then, I will summarize the Roman Catholic teaching on justification. To accomplish this task, I will consider the Council of Trent's "Decree Concerning Justification," the most even-handed and representative Church pronouncement on the issue to date. I will also consider a wide array of Catholic authors, both past and present.[2]

The Roman Catholic Teaching

Our study of the Roman Catholic doctrine of justification begins, as the Council of Trent suggests, with a discussion of original sin.[3] The Council states:

> The holy council declares first, that for a correct and clear understanding of the doctrine of justification, it is necessary that each one recognize and confess that…all men had lost innocence in the prevarication of Adam, having become unclean, and, as the Apostle says, by nature children of wrath. (Sess. VI, Chap. I)

Adam's sin involved the loss of his supernatural status as a son of God.[4] The Roman Catholic doctrine of justification, therefore, is concerned essentially with "the restoration of that justice which Adam possessed prior to his sin, and which he loses by his sin."[5] The Council of Trent itself summarizes the justification of the sinner as "a translation from that state in which man is born a child of the first Adam, to the state of grace and of the adoption of the sons of God through the second Adam, Jesus Christ, our Savior." (Sess. VI, Chap. IV)

As an outcast estranged from God's family, the sinner can do nothing to merit justification; he is dead in sin and in need of God's grace. The sola gratia then, is an integral aspect of the Catholic doctrine of justification,[6] and is clearly affirmed by Trent, "…we are therefore said to be justified gratuitously, because none of those things that precede justification, whether faith or works, merit the grace of justification." (Sess. VI, Chap. VIII) It is impossible for man, as a sinner, to contribute anything to his justification; it is purely gratuitous.[7]

Grace then, enables individuals to have faith,[8] repent, and be baptized.[9] Trent states:

Now, they (the adults) are disposed to that justice when, aroused and aided by divine grace, receiving faith by hearing, they are moved freely toward God, believing to be true what has been divinely revealed and promised… and they begin to love Him as the fountain of all justice, and on that account are moved against sin by a certain hatred and detestation, that is, by that repentance that must be performed before baptism; finally…they resolve to receive baptism, to begin a new life and to keep the commandments of God. (Sess. VI, Chap. VI)

In this process, the sacrament of baptism is the instrumental cause (Sess. VI, Chap. VII) of justification.[10] In baptism, the sinner is endowed with new qualities,[11] and passes from a state of enmity towards God to a state of grace; he is adopted into God's family as a son. In short, justification in the Catholic view is the gift of divine sonship, lost in original sin, and regained in Christ.

Justification understood in this way involves both the imputation of sonship and the infusion of Christ's grace. These two aspects are inseparable, for as God imputes family standing to the sinner, the sinner does in fact become a member of the family; sonship is no legal fiction.[12] God effectuates what He declares.

Hence, when God declares the sinner righteous, it is more than a mere legal declaration. It is a creative and transformative action whereby God takes someone and breathes into Him that Spirit of sonship which cries, "Abba!" "Father!"[13] Gratuitous, therefore, means more than the receipt of divine favor. What God imparts in the gift of grace is Himself, nothing less, and this life-giving divine gift is a metaphysical, ontological communication of Christ's sonship.[14]

This internal renovation is essential. For individuals are both imputed with Adam's guilt and infused with his corrupt nature; they are declared sinful, and at the same time, they really are sinful. Hence, justified persons are both imputed with Christ's righteousness and infused with His life;[15] they are declared righteous because, in virtue of Christ's indwelling life and holiness, they really are righteous.[16] The remission of sins is possible because the grace of Christ is infused into the person, making him a child of God. By virtue of this new filial relationship, the individual is no longer subject to the wrath of God.[17]

God's judgment then is directed towards a child in the second Adam, and not a rebel criminal in the first Adam. This helps explain why justified persons need not be perfect themselves; they are justified by virtue of their new relationship to God as sons. The judgment is taking place then with regard to Christ's grace alive in the individual, at whatever degree of growth; the indwelling grace of Christ justifies sinners.[18]

In this study, we have referred to God's grace in several different ways. First of all, the supernatural enlightenment of the understanding, enabling people to shun evil and do good, is called "actual grace".[19] An initial act of faith, for example, is a result of "actual grace." We have also seen that "grace is an inward gift communicated by God to the soul, in virtue of which man is made holy and pleasing to God, a child of God, and heir of heaven."[20] This abiding quality in the soul is called "habitual" or "sanctifying grace."[21]

As long as the individual retains this grace, he remains justified.[22] Now this grace is nothing less than the presence of God in the soul.[23] For as we have seen, grace is an abundant provision, an ontological substance, and not just a subjective attitude of favor.

The justified person continually seeks to obtain this grace. The Council of Trent states:

> Having, therefore, been justified and made the friends and domestics of God...they, through the observance of the commandments of God and of the Church, faith cooperating with good works, increase in that justice received through the grace of Christ and are further justified, as it is written: He that is just, let him be justified still. (Sess. VI, Chap. X)

Understood in this way, it is clear that justification is a process, and not merely a once and for all act.[24] The sinner is reborn as a son of God. After the birth process, however, the Father expects for that life to be nurtured, to be cultivated by the son. In other words, the Father has not simply given sonship as a welfare check; He has given life that is to be lived out. The inheritance of salvation is then the natural culmination of lifelong growth in filial dependence, obedience, and maturity, all of which require the subsequent cooperation of the regenerated person with God's operating grace.

"Sanctifying grace" is precisely the means by which the children of God "grow up," so to speak. We have seen how this grace is infused in individuals through baptism when they are first justified, incorporating them into God's family. Simply put, the rest of the sacraments[25] (especially the Eucharist) are covenantal dispensers of divine grace,[26] whereby the children of God receive spiritual food to help them further mature in the family.[27] Inasmuch as the justified person continually seeks to obtain this grace through the sacraments and by doing good works, justification is indeed by works.[28] The *sola fide* then, is not a part of Catholic doctrine.[29]

One effect of "sanctifying grace" is the power of merit, i.e., the capacity to win heaven as a reward. Now, if grace is gratuitous (as its name indicates), and merit is an effect of grace, then merit too is gratuitous. But how is this so? As a plethora of biblical passages indicate, there is a direct connection between works performed and an individual's future standing in heaven.[30] Simply put, this is God's free promise to the justified person to reward his actions when that person obeys His commands.[31] When God rewards meritorious works, therefore, He is simply crowning His own achievements in the justified person as a result of the Holy Spirit working in him.[32] As Augustine states, "When He rewards man He rewards only His own gifts."

Summary and Conclusion

Due to the limitations of time and space, I must draw this study to a close. To summarize, we saw that the original justice, or the divine sonship, of Adam was lost through original sin. Justification, in the Catholic sense, is the restoration of that sonship through the second Adam, Jesus Christ; sinners are reborn through baptism as sons of God. In this process, justification is purely gratuitous. The Holy Spirit works in the sinner, effectuating in him an orientation towards faith and good works. Through baptism, he is imputed standing in God's family and infused with Christ's grace.

Justification then, involves both the legal remission and the actual removal of sin. The forgiveness of sins is possible precisely because the justified person stands in a new relationship to God as a son. Because the grace of Christ is in him, original sin is blotted out, actual sins are remitted, and grace is continually imparted to overcome concupiscence. The justified person continually seeks to obtain "sanctifying grace" through the sacraments (which in the case of adults, are useless without real faith) and by doing good works. In this sense, individuals are justified by works as well as faith, but always by grace alone and Christ alone. Justification is a process, therefore, whereby higher standing is progressively conferred upon children growing up.

Finally, we saw that one of the benefits of being in a state of grace is the ability to merit the reward of heaven. God is a faithful father, promising to reward the good works of justified persons. In doing so, He crowns his own achievements, for even the most pious saint is ever dependent on God's grace.

As I stated in the introduction, a critical evaluation of the Catholic view is beyond the scope of this study. Yet, I think a few brief comments are in order. First of all, this study has forced me to abandon some false notions I have had for some time now, including my belief that Roman Catholic doctrine and the *sola gratia* are mutually exclusive. Furthermore, the stereotypical picture of Catholicism (among evangelicals) is that of a legalistic system unconcerned with saving faith in Christ. While this may be true sometimes in practice, it has no place in the actual teaching of the Catholic Church.

Secondly, I find appealing the way in which Roman Catholics explain justification through the covenant family idea,[33] without ignoring the imputative legal aspect. In fact, the imputative aspect is naturally explained within the framework of the covenant family. In the natural realm, a father imputes family standing to his newborn son, not on the basis of any works done on the son's part, but because of the seed of sonship alive in the son as a result of the father. In the same way, God the Father declares us to be heirs in His supernatural family. But just as the birth process in the natural realm, God expects His children to grow up, and, He is glorified in raising them up in His likeness, making them stronger and wiser. The inheritance of eternal life, therefore, is the reward of filial obedience and maturity. This in essence, is the Roman Catholic doctrine of justification. The strongest case for the Catholic view is made by those who explain justification in this way, and yet, paradoxically, many Catholics themselves seem unaware of the covenant family paradigm.[34]

On the negative side, I still, as a Calvinist, affirm the notion of the perseverance of the saints. Yet, it is clear that in the Catholic view, the threat of losing one's salvation and falling out of a state of grace is very real. I must confess, however, that this misgiving is made without really having made an effort to understand the Catholics on this point. Indeed, the Catholic doctrine of grace is very complex; I have only scratched the surface in this essay. Further study on this important issue, I think, would prove fruitful for evangelicals.

About Richard A. White

Richard White composed this paper in 1987 while a seminary student at Trinity Evangelical Divinity School (TEDS).

Richard completed his doctoral work at Marquette. The title of his dissertation was "Justification in Ecumenical Dialogue: An Assessment of the Catholic Contribution" (1995). He converted to Catholicism while at Marquette. Dr. White is currently the chair of the Theology Department at Benedictine College in Atchison, KS.

Glossary for Studying Justification by Faith

The words below are theological terms you need to know in order to understand justification and the various doctrines connected with it. These terms (except for *imputation*) are described from a Catholic viewpoint.

You'll discover that several of the terms are interconnected. The definitions of some terms appearing later in the list are helpful in understanding terms listed earlier; therefore, going through the Glossary at least twice is recommended.

Adoption refers to the justified believer becoming a child of God. Transformed by divine grace, the adopted son of God enjoys much more than the title and the external status of a child of God. The person actually becomes God's child, sharing the divine life of the Trinity in the New Covenant. The Spirit of adoption, the Holy Spirit, in the heart of the believer cries out, "Abba, Father," witnessing to the nearly unimaginable blessing of being a child of God. Adoption in Catholic teaching is an important facet of the life of the justified believer.

Note: Protestants believe in adoption and emphasize it to varying degrees, but they are careful to distinguish and separate adoption from justification.

Baptism is the sacrament of faith that unites a person with Christ, who died for our sins and rose for our justification. The believer receives the remission of original and personal sin. By Baptism, the faithful are born anew (regenerated) by water and the Spirit. This spiritual birth as a child of God is the beginning of a new life as an adopted child of God.

Imputation is a term that describes the external righteousness in the Protestant understanding of justification. The "righteousness" given in the Protestant doctrine of justification is an external, legal (forensic) declaration of "not guilty." Protestants do not believe that the righteousness imputed in justification works any internal change in the believer. Protestants do believe in regeneration, sanctification, and adoption, but as separate and distinct works of grace related to, but not directly involved with, justification.

Infusion is the important term Catholics use to describe the profound internal work of grace in justification which makes the person inwardly righteous (not just externally declared righteous). The infusion of grace enables the believer to share a new life in union with the Blessed Trinity as a child of God. The infusion of grace in justification is thus related to sanctification, and adoption.

Justification refers to God making sinners righteous. It is the gracious act of God which profoundly transforms an unjust person into a just person. Justification transforms a sinful descendant of Adam into a righteous child of God. The believer is not just declared righteous, but actually made inwardly righteous by an infusion of sanctifying grace. The justified person is interiorly renewed. In the words of St. Paul, he is a "new creation."

Justification includes an inward removal of sin, regeneration, sanctification, and adoption. Initial justification is by faith and baptism, yet justification is a lifelong process. Ongoing justification is not by faith alone, but by faith working through love.

Greek and English Terms for "justification" and "faith"

In the Greek New Testament there are three related words (a noun, an adjective, and a verb) stemming from a single Greek root that expresses righteousness. English translations often have two ways to translate the Greek root word:

	Greek	**Strong's #**[103]	**English**
Noun	*dikaiŏsunē*	1343	justification, righteousness
Adjective	*dikaios*	1342	just, righteous
Verb	*dikaiŏō*	1344	to justify, to make righteous

Similarly, there are often two English words used to translate a single Greek root word for belief/believing:

	Greek	**Strong's #**	**English**
Noun	*pistis*	4102	belief, faith
Adjective	*pistŏs*	4103	believing, faithful
Verb	*pistĕuŏ*	4100	to believe, to have faith

Examples from important "justification by faith" passages in Romans and Galatians:

For I am not ashamed of the gospel: it is the power of God for salvation to every one who has faith, to the Jew first and also to the Greek. For in it the *righteousness* of God is revealed through faith for faith; as it is written, "He who through faith is *righteous* shall live." (Rom 1:16 –17; my italics)

Thus Abraham "believed God, and it was reckoned to him as righteousness." So you see that it is men of faith who are the sons of Abraham. And the scripture, foreseeing that God would justify the Gentiles by faith, preached the gospel beforehand to Abraham … (Gal 3:6–8; my italics)

Merit is a gracious divine reward for good works performed by a justified person in a state of grace, and this grace precedes, accompanies, and follows the act that merits. The *Catechism* says, "The source of any merit we have before God is due to the grace of Christ in us."[104] According to St. Augustine, the reward of merit is God crowning his own gifts of grace.

The **New Perspective** is a ground-breaking interpretation of St. Paul's polemic against those trying to enforce the "works of the law" upon Gentile converts. Historical research has demonstrated that first-century Judaism *wasn't* a legalistic religion of self-righteousness. If this is true, then what was it that Paul so fiercely opposed in his Epistles? He opposed requiring Gentile converts to practice distinctive Jewish observances (such as food laws, circumcision, and Jewish holy days) in order to be accepted as full members of the Christian community. Three Protestant scholars, E. P. Sanders, James D. G. Dunn, and N. T. Wright have been influential in the spread of the New Perspective. The term "New Perspective" was first used by Dunn in 1982.

Pelagianism refers to a group heretical errors originating from the monk Pelagius (A.D. 354–425). Pelagianism is the heretical theory which teaches man is capable of a type of "do-it-yourself salvation," in effect denying the necessity of grace for salvation. St. Augustine and St. Jerome strongly opposed Pelagius, insisting on the necessity of the grace of God for salvation. Pelagius' teaching was formally condemned as heresy by the Catholic Church at the Council of Carthage in A.D. 418. Pelagius was subsequently banished from Rome. Although Pelagianism was forcefully condemned by the Catholic Church, Luther and other reformers claimed that Catholic doctrine was Pelagian.

Regeneration being born again as a child of God, as a result of faith and baptism.

Sanctification means being made holy and righteous. Sanctification describes the effects of sanctifying grace, i.e., the righteousness infused with justification. Sanctification begins with Baptism, but it also involves an ongoing component, perfecting the life of the believer into the likeness of Christ. The lifelong process of growing in likeness to Christ is sometimes termed by Catholics "second sanctification."

WORKS is a term that when used alone can be misunderstood. Catholics distinguish between "works of the law" and "good works."

Works of the law are traditionally understood to be human efforts, unaided by grace, seeking to obtain righteousness (i.e., justification) and a right standing with God. St. Paul's harshest criticisms fall upon the "works of the law." In the New Perspective, "works of the law" are understood to be those distinctive Jewish practices that separated Jews from Gentiles.

Good works are those human efforts that are inspired and energized by the Holy Spirit. St. Paul and St. James both insist on the necessity of good works for the believer since genuine faith always is working through love. Good works are not the basis of initial justification, but are always present in the life of one justified and transformed by grace.

Endnotes

1. My Introduction to Justification by God's Grace

[1]For a brief description of Pelagianism, see John A. Hardon, *Pocket Catholic Dictionary* (New York: Doubleday, 1985), 319, or online at http://www.catholicculture.org/culture/library/dictionary/index.cfm?id=35492.For a detailed explanation, see the article on Pelagius and Pelagianism in the Catholic Encyclopedia at http://www.newadvent.org/cathen/11604a.htm.

[2] Italics in the original; bold emphasis added.

[3] What is an Evangelical Protestant? There are three general types of Protestants: mainline, Fundamentalist, and Evangelical. The *mainline* denominations tend to be theologically liberal, with a strong emphasis on social justice, and have accommodated themselves to progressive moral values such as being "pro-choice" on abortion and accepting same-sex marriage. The mainline denominations are represented by such groups as the United Methodist Church, Presbyterian Church USA, the Episcopal Church, and the Evangelical Lutheran Church (which despite using the designation "Evangelical" is in reality a mainline denomination). *Fundamentalism* was a conservative reaction to the growing theological liberalism and secular social- justice outlook in mainline denominations. The movement began among conservative Presbyterians in the late 19th century and soon spread to conservatives among the Baptists and other denominations rejecting theological modernism. The contemporary *Evangelical* movement arose in the mid-twentieth century out of Fundamentalism with an emphasis on traditional Reformation doctrines, vigorous engagement in evangelism and missions, while seeking to be intellectually relevant and engaged in social justice issues. Evangelical churches, while considerably diverse, may be independent congregations, or ones attached to newer offshoots from liberal denominations. For example, the Presbyterian Church in America (PCA), my former denomination and ministerial affiliation, is an Evangelical denomination holding traditional Calvinistic Reformation beliefs in contrast with the more liberal Presbyterian Church USA.

[4] There are several variations in the Protestant understandings of justification and interpretations of the Epistle to the Romans. For the sake of brevity,

I'll be presenting the Protestant position in a singular fashion, somewhat generically, without referencing all the various nuances and differences between Protestant groups.

⁵ John Calvin, Prefatory Address to Francis I, King of France, in *Institutes of the Christian Religion*, no. 4, trans. Ford Lewis Battles (Philadelphia: Westminster Press, 1960), 18.

2. How to Discover What Catholics Really Believe

⁶ John Paul II, Apostolic Constitution on the Publication of the "Catechism of the Catholic Church" *Fidei Depositum* (Oct. 11, 1992), no. 3, in *Catechism of the Catholic Church: Revised in Accordance with the Official Latin Text Promulgated by Pope John Paul II*, 2nd ed. (Washington, DC, and Vatican City: United States Conference of Catholic Bishops–Libreria Editrice Vaticana, 1997), p. 5.

⁷ Joseph Cardinal Ratzinger and Christoph Schönborn, *Introduction to the "Catechism of the Catholic Church"* (San Francisco: Ignatius Press, 1994), 48–49.

⁸ Ibid., 90.

⁹ Ibid., 91.

¹⁰ Ibid., 48.

¹¹ *The Canons and Decrees of the Council of Trent*, trans. Rev. H. J. Schroeder (Rockford, IL: TAN, 1978). The online edition of Session 6 of the Council of Trent (concerning justification) can be found at http://www.ewtn.com/library/councils/trent6.htm. (All twenty-five sessions of the council are also available online, at http://www.ewtn.com/library/indexes/COUNCILS.htm, no. 61.)

¹² *Catechism of the Catholic Church* (hereinafter referred to in notes as *CCC*), no. 1994; italics in the original. (References to the *CCC* are given in paragraph numbers rather than page numbers.)

¹³ St. Thomas Aquinas, *Summa Theologica* Ia–IIae, q. 113, a. 9.

¹⁴ Canon F. Cuttaz, *Our Life of Grace* (Chicago: Fides Publishers Association, 1958), 36.

¹⁵ Collin Hansen, "*Not* All Evangelicals and Catholics Together: Protestant Debate on Justification Is Reigniting Questions about Rome," *Christianity Today*, Nov. 2009.

[16] John Paul II, *Fidei Depositum,* no. 3; *CCC*, pp. 5–6. Emphasis added.

[17] Peter Kreeft, *Fundamentals of the Faith: Essays in Christian Apologetics* (San Francisco: Ignatius Press, 1988), 290. In 1989 Dr. Kreeft admitted that his statements regarding *sola fide* in *Fundamentals* were "misleading." Unfortunately, the erroneous statements in Kreeft's book were still in print at the time of the writing of the present work. I know Peter Kreeft to be a good man, justly held in high regard for the fine work he has done over the years. And to be fair, on p. 291, Kreeft does give some explanation of the divergent understandings Protestants and Catholics have of key terms. However, there may be other readers besides myself who would not find this sufficient to clarify his previous statements.

3. What Does the Term "Justification" Mean?

[18] Council of Trent, Session 6, Decree on Justification (Jan. 13, 1547), chap. 4.

[19] This definition isn't complete from either a Catholic or Protestant viewpoint, but it is a working definition enabling us to launch into the topic.

[20] Italics added.

[21] John Henry Newman, *Lectures on the Doctrine of Justification* (London: Longmans, Green and Co., 1914), 335.

[22] *CCC*, glossary: "justification," p. 885; cf. also *CCC*, nos. 1987–89.

4. Justification: By Faith, or by Faith Alone?

[23] Protestants and Catholics also have differing concepts of the faith that justifies. Protestants believe that *fiducial* (trusting) faith is the crucial act, by which a person trustfully commits himself to the mercy of God. Catholic theologian Ludwig Ott, describing the content of justifying faith, says, "The so-called fiducial faith does not suffice. What is demanded is theological or dogmatic faith (*confessional* faith) which consists in the firm acceptance of the Divine truths of Revelation, on the authority of God Revealing." Ludwig Ott, *Fundamentals of Catholic Dogma*, (Rockford, IL: TAN, 1969), 253. Therefore, Catholics must believe all the truths revealed by God both in Scripture and Sacred Tradition and as is confessed in summary form in the creeds.

[24] Council of Trent, Session 6, Decree on Justification, chap. 8.

[25] Council of Trent, Session 6, Canons concerning Justification, canon 9.

[26] Morton H. Smith, Ph.D., "Justification: The Key to Our Acceptance with God," *Katekōmen* 14, no. 1 (2003): 6, citing Michael S. Horton, "Are We Justified by Faith Alone?—What Still Divides Us: A Protestant & Roman Catholic Debate," http://graceonlinelibrary.org/doctrine-theology/justification/are-we-justified-by-faith-alone-what-still-divides-us-a-protestant-roman-catholic-debate-by-michael-s-horton/.

[27] R. C. Sproul, *Faith Alone: The Evangelical Doctrine of Justification* (Grand Rapids: Zondervan, 1995), 36.

[28] Martin Luther, quoted in Henry O'Connor, *Luther's Own Statements concerning His Teaching and Its Results: Taken Exclusively from the Earliest and Best Editions of Luther's German and Latin Works* (New York: Benziger, 1884), 25-26.

[29] Ibid., 25.

5. What Happens When We Are Justified?

[30] R. C. Sproul, "Justification by Faith Alone (The Forensic Nature of Justification)," in *Justification by Faith Alone: Affirming the Doctrine by Which the Church and the Individual Stands or Falls*, by John Mac Arthur, R. C. Sproul, Joel Beeke, John Gerstner, and John Armstrong (Morgan, PA: Soli Deo Gloria Publications, 1995), 29.

[31] Congregation for the Doctrine of the Faith and the Pontifical Council for Promoting Christian Unity, Response of the Catholic Church to the Joint Declaration of the Catholic Church and the Lutheran World Federation on the Doctrine of Justification (June 25, 1998), no. 1. Available online at http://www.vatican.va/roman_curia/pontifical_councils/chrstuni/documents/rc_pc_chrstuni_doc_01081998_off-answer-catholic_en.html.

[32] Ibid., no. 4.

[33] "The Joint Declaration between the Catholic Church and the Lutheran World Federation on the Doctrine of Justification," *L'Osservatore Romano*, Jan. 26, 2002, 9–10.

[34] Ibid.

[35] See the brief description of justification in the Council of Trent, Session 6, Decree on Justification, chap. 4.

[36] Ott, *Fundamentals of Catholic Dogma*, 251 (see chap. 4, n. 1, above).

6. Justification, Baptism, and Sanctification

[37] Council of Trent, Session 6, Decree on Justification, chap. 7.

[38] *CCC*, no. 1987.

[39] Hardon, *Pocket Catholic Dictionary*, 393 (see chap. 1, n. 1, above).

[40] Gerhard Kittel and Gerhard Friedrich, eds., *Theological Dictionary of the New Testament*, translated and abridged in one volume by Geoffrey W. Bromiley (Grand Rapids: Eerdmans, 1985), 539.

[41] St. Augustine, *The City of God* 22.8, in *The Nicene and Post-Nicene Fathers*, vol. 2, ed. Philip Schaff (Grand Rapids: Eerdmans, 1983), 487.

[42] St. John Chrysostom, "Homily XI, Epistle to the Romans 6:5," in *Nicene and Post-Nicene Fathers*, 11:408.

[43] *CCC*, no. 1987, referencing Rom 6.

[44] Many Evangelicals question baptizing infants. They may ask, "How can infants believe?" The *Catechism* teaches that children baptized in infancy have to be instructed in the faith after Baptism so that they may grow up believing (no. 1231). The *Catechism* also teaches that neither children nor adults have a mature faith at Baptism, so they both have a necessity to grow in the faith (nos. 1253–54). Finally, the *Catechism* states that "the grace of salvation bestowed on infants is particularly manifest in infant Baptism" (no. 1250).

[45] *CCC*, no. 1992; italics in the original.

[46] For references in the *Catechism* pertaining to justification, sanctification, and Baptism, see nos. 1987, 1989, 1991–92, 1995, 1997, 2003, 2019–20. Also see Council of Trent, Session 6, Decree on Justification, chap. 7.

[47] *CCC*, no. 1997.

[48]

7. Adoption: The Crown of Justification

J. I. Packer, *Knowing God* (Downers Grove, IL: InterVarsity Press, 1973), 182.

[49] Ott, *Fundamentals of Catholic Dogma*, 258 (see chap. 4, n. 1, above).

⁵⁰ Council of Trent, Session 6, Decree on Justification, chap. 4.

⁵¹ Even much of Romans 12-15 is devoted to the practical application of New Covenant relations between Jew and Gentile as a result of both groups being justified by faith.

⁵² Msgr. F. Cuttaz, *Children of God* (Notre Dame, IN: Fides Publishers, 1963), 5–6.

⁵³ *CCC*, nos. 1996–97; italics in the original.

8. Seeing "Good Works" through the Lens of Adoption

⁵⁴ Cuttaz, *Children of God*, 5.

⁵⁵ See *CCC,* no. 1814, and Gal 5:6.

⁵⁶ F. F. Bruce, *Paul: Apostle of the Heart Set Free* (Grand Rapids: Eerdmans, 1978), 19 and 21, citing the frequently quoted words of Thomas Erskine.

⁵⁷ For an example of a knowledgeable Evangelical theologian and Scripture scholar quoting only Ephesians 2:8–9 and ignoring Ephesians 2:10 while discussing Catholic beliefs on good works, see Wayne Grudem's *Systematic Theology: An Introduction to Biblical Doctrine* (Grand Rapids: Zondervan, 1994), 730–31. Dr. Grudem uses the Ephesians 2:8–9 tactic twice within the space of two pages, trying to infer that Catholics believe in salvation by "works of the law." In the same section, Dr. Grudem also gives an isolated reference to Titus 3:7 to bolster his argument without referencing Titus 3:8. Ask yourself, "Why would a scholar so familiar with these Scriptures fail to include adjacent verses so pertinent to the works question?"

⁵⁸ Council of Trent, Session 6, Decree on Justification, chap. 16; emphasis added.

9. Merit: Gracious Rewards from the Father

⁵⁹ Council of Trent, Session 6, Decree on Justification, chap. 16.

⁶⁰ *CCC*, nos. 2008–9, citing St. Augustine. Italics in the original; bold emphasis added.

⁶¹ *CCC*, no. 2011; italics in the original.

⁶² *CCC*, no. 306.

10. Can I Lose My Justification?

[63] *CCC*, no. 1857.

[64] Council of Trent, Session 6, Decree on Justification, chap. 4.

[65] John Paul II, *Crossing the Threshold of Hope*, ed. Vittorio Messori (New York: Alfred A. Knopf Publishers, 1994), 227–28; italics in the original.

[66] *CCC*, glossary: "mortal sin"; cf. nos. 1855, 1857.

[67] Hardon, *Pocket Catholic Dictionary*, p. 344 (see chap. 1, n. 1, above)..

[68] *CCC*, nos. 1077—83, 1110.

[69] *CCC*, no. 1098.

11. New Perspectives on St. Paul

[70] The following are books for each of the three leading Protestant authors on the New Perspective. Sanders' easy-to-understand book draws out the implications of the New Perspective with a strong repudiation of Luther's views of justification. Wright's book contains some of the best New Perspective scholarship with medium difficulty. Dunn's books are advanced, but rewarding reading.

E. P. Sanders, *Paul: A Very Short Introduction* (New York: Oxford University Press, 2001).

N. T. Wright, *What Saint Paul Really Said: Was Paul of Tarsus the Real Founder of Christianity?* (Grand Rapids: William B. Eerdmans, 1997).

James D. G. Dunn, *The New Perspective on Paul*, rev. ed. (Grand Rapids: William B. Eerdmans, 2008).

———. *The Theology of Paul the Apostle* (Grand Rapids: William B. Eerdmans, 1998).

[71] *CCC,* no. 1996.

[72] For an excellent example of a synthesis of the traditional perspective and the New Perspective, see Michael J. Gorman, *Reading Paul* (Eugene, OR: Cascade Books, 2008).

12. Justification and Divinization by Grace

[73] St. Augustine, *On the Gospel of John* 72.3, cited in *CCC*, no. 1994.

[74] St. Thomas Aquinas, *Summa Theologica* IaIIae, q. 113 a. 9.

[75] John Henry Newman, *Lectures on the Doctrine of Justification* (London: Longmans, Green and Co., 1914), 335.

[76] *CCC,* no. 2019. Also see nos. 1989 and 1995.

[77] Council of Trent, Session 6, Decree on Justification, chap. 4; and *CCC*, nos. 1996–97.

[78] *CCC*, nos. 1996, 1997, 1999 (citing 2 Cor 5:17–18), and 1988 (citing St. Athanasius, *Epistle to Serapionem,* 1.24). Italics in the original.

[79] Clark H. Pinnock, *Flame of Love: A Theology of the Holy Spirit* (Downers Grove, IL: InterVarsity Press Academic, 1996), 100–101, 81, 156.

[80] For instance, in his commentary on Paul's statement in Romans that we are to be "conformed" (Gk. *symmorphous*) to Christ, C. E. B. Cranfield states that this process begins in this life: "It is probable that Paul is here [Rom 8] thinking not only of their final glorification but also of their growing conformity to Christ here and now in suffering and in obedience. *Symmorphous* is meant to embrace sanctification as well as final glory … so as a progressive renewal of the believer into that likeness of God. Though final glorification is still future … their glorification has already been accomplished in Christ …The fact that sanctification is not mentioned as an intermediate link between justification and glorification … [may be because] *edoxasen*, ("glorified") covered sanctification as well as glorification, since there is a real sense in which it is a beginning of glorification (cf. 2 Cor 3:18). Verse 29 [*symmorphous*] referred not only to conformity to Christ's glory hereafter but also to being conformed to Him here and now." C. E. B. Cranfield, *The International Critical Commentary: A Critical and Exegetical Commentary on Romans*, vol. 1 (Edinburgh: T&T Clark Ltd. 1975), 432–33.

[81] Scott Hahn, foreword to *Called to be the Children of God: The Catholic Theology of Human Deification*, ed. David Meconi and Carl E. Olson (San Francisco: Ignatius Press, 2016), 9.

[82] *CCC*, no. 460; italics in the original.

[83] St. Irenaeus, *Against Heresies* 3.19.1, cited in *CCC*, no. 460. Also found in *Nicene and Post-Nicene Fathers*, 1:448 (see chap. 6, n. 5, above).

84 St. Athanasius, *On the Incarnation* 54.3, cited in *CCC*, no. 460.

85 St. Augustine, *On the Psalms* 50.2, in *Nicene and Post-Nicene Fathers*, 8:178.

86 Ibid.

87 St. Augustine, *On the Trinity* 13.9, in *Nicene and Post-Nicene Fathers*, 3:174.

88 St. Athanasius, *Letter to Serapion*, cited in *CCC*, no. 1988.

89 John Paul II, Apostolic Letter *Orientale Lumen* (*The Light of the East*), May 2, 1995, no. 6.

90 *CCC*, no. 1127.

91 John Calvin, *Calvin's New Testament Commentaries*, vol. 12, on 2 Pet 1:3. Available online at http://www.ccel.org/ccel/calvin/calcom45.vii.ii.i.html.

92 Pinnock, *Flame of Love,* 154–56.

93 William Sanday and Arthur Headlam, *A Critical and Exegetical Commentary on the Epistle to the Romans* (Edinburgh: T&T Clark, 1902), 218.

94 C. S. Lewis, *Mere Christianity* (New York: Macmillan, 1943), 174, 182, 185, 187.

95 C. S. Lewis, *The Weight of Glory* (New York, Macmillan, 1949), 13.

96 Ibid.

Appendix I: Ecumenical Documents on Justification

97 Second Vatican Council, Decree on Ecumenism, *Unitatis Redintegratio*, Nov. 21, 1964, no. 1. http://www.vatican.va/archive/hist_councils/ii_vatican_council/documents/vat-ii_decree_19641121_unitatis-redintegratio_en.html.

98 The document is also called "ECT II" (for Evangelicals and Catholics Together II), since "The Gift of Salvation" was a follow-up to an earlier document entitled "Evangelicals and Catholics Together: The Christian Mission in the Third Millennium," published in May 1994.

99 Dr. John H. Armstrong, "Evangelical and Catholics Together: A New

Initiative or Further Confusion?" *Viewpoint* 2, no. 1 (Jan-Feb 1998), http://the-highway.com/ECT_Armstrong.html.

[100] *The Religion and Society Report*, July 1998.

[101] Randy Frame, "Evangelicals, Catholics Issue Salvation Accord," *Christianity Today,* Jan. 12, 1998, http://www.christianitytoday.com/ct/1998/january12/8t1061.html?start=1.

[102] Gene Edward Veith, "On Earth Peace?" *WORLD Magazine*, Dec. 25, 1999, https://world.wng.org/1999/12/on_earth_peace.

Appendix II: Sola Gratia, Solo Christo: The Roman Catholic Doctrine of Justification

[1] James Buchanan, *The Doctrine of Justification* (London: The Banner of Truth Trust, 1961), p. 226.

[2] My goal is to set forth the Catholic position, not to critique it. Thus, I will not preface my remarks with such phrases as "the Catholic position says" or "in Rome's view." The reader should assume that all of the text represents the Catholic teaching. Now the Catholic view of grace and justification is very complex. Due to the scope of this essay, therefore, many subject areas (e.g., metaphysical questions, purgatory, indulgences, the mode of God's indwelling in the soul, etc.) relating to the Catholic teaching on justification have been excluded. The reader should consult the footnotes, however, for elaboration on certain points.

[3] For a Roman Catholic treatment, see A.M. Dubarle, *The Biblical Doctrine of Original Sin* (New York: Herder and Herder, 1964).

[4] Matthias J. Scheeben, an eminent German Roman Catholic theologian of the 19th century, explains, "It is a complete estrangement and separation of man from God as his supernatural end, and is met with on God's part not by a simple displeasure—involving disfavor in the moral sense—but by a forcible ejection from the state of the children of God, a stripping away of the supernatural raiment of grace." In short, the divine sonship of Adam was lost thru original sin.

[5] Ibid., pp. 614-615.

[6] The Council of Orange, in condemning the Pelagian and semi-Pelagian heresies, states, "If anyone asserts that we can, by our natural powers, think as we ought, or choose any good pertaining to the salvation of eternal life,

that is, consent to salvation or to the message of the Gospel, without the illumination and inspiration of the Holy Spirit, who gives to all men facility in assenting to and believing the truth; he is misled by a heretical spirit..." (Canon 7) For a good discussion of the Catholic teaching, see Louis Bouyer, *The Spirit and Forms of Protestantism* (Westminster, Maryland: The Newman Press, 1956), pp. 43-58.

[7] Michael Schmaus, a Catholic dogmatician, sums it up nicely, "Man needs something, as vital to him as his daily bread, which he himself cannot earn. Grace is for him a matter of life and death; yet he cannot obtain it through his own efforts. Thus he must learn that grace is a gift. The ultimate reason for this is that God is absolute transcendence, and no amount of effort or exertion on man's part can bring God within his grasp." *Justification and the Last Things* (Kansas City: Sheed and Ward, 1977), p. 21.

[8] Trent states, "...we are therefore said to be justified by faith, because faith is the beginning of human salvation, the foundation and root of all justification, without which it is impossible to please God and come to the fellowship of sons..." (Sess. VI, Chap. VIII)

[9] In the case of the infant, "the process has simply the character of an ineffable, supernatural generation, to the exclusion of all cooperation between the person generated and his begetter. With adults the case is different... Hence the grace which comes down from above is met by an ascent from below; the descent of the supernatural into nature is matched by an effort of the latter to raise itself. In this case also the activity of God, regarded in its power and efficacy as the communication of supernatural existence and life, remains a true generation." Scheeben, *The Mysteries of Christianity*, p. 633.

[10] Emile Mersch S.J. states, "In the order of logical succession, the first effect of baptism will be the destruction of original sin and all other sins. By joining a man to the Church, the sacrament joins him to Christ in His union with men, that is, to Christ who gives Himself to mankind in His passion and in the Mass. And Christ who thus gives Himself is Christ who destroys original sin and all sins. By uniting us to Christ finally, baptism unites us to the Son, to God, to the Trinity; it incorporates us into Christ and confers on us divine adoption, grace, the supernatural life, and the indwelling of the whole Trinity." *The Theology of the Mystical Body* (St. Louis: B. Herder Book Co., 1951), pp. 561-61.

[11] The three theological virtues, faith, hope, and love are infused into the soul. Schmaus states, "...in the divine act of justification man is given the capacity for a divinizing life in faith, hope, and love. Actually this teach-

ing of the Council of Trent does not differ from the idea of regeneration put forward by the Reformers, which refers simply to the justifying action of God himself in man." *Justification and the Last Things*, p. 83. In Calvinist doctrine, regeneration leads to faith, which in turn leads to justification. Thus, justification is preceded by an infusion of new qualities, i.e., an inner transformation which produces in the individual an orientation towards faith and works. The Calvinist then, finds himself in the same camp with the Catholics in placing regeneration before justification in the order of salvation. To many Lutherans, this amounts to denying the *sola fide*. If justification depends on an inner transformation, then it is no longer justification by faith alone. See for example, Edward Boehl, *The Reformed Doctrine of Justification* (Grand Rapids, Michigan: Eerdmans, 1946), pp. 195-196; Robert Brinsmead, "Further Observations on the Order of Justification and Regeneration," *Present Truth* 5/6 (September 1976), p. 17. Also of importance is the Norman Shepherd controversy at Westminster Seminary in Philadelphia. The views of Professor Shepherd were vigorously debated because he did not make clear the distinction between faith and works in justification. He maintained that inasmuch as they are both the result of God's regenerating work, there is no warrant for separating them; they are both equally necessary for justification (even if faith is given priority). Professor Shepherd eventually left Westminster because of the controversy.

[12] Canon F. Cuttaz states, "With God, no abstraction or fiction is possible. He does not call anyone His child unless He has made him His child. He does not love anyone with a Father's love unless he is really His son." *Our Life of Grace* (Chicago, Illinois: Fides Publishers Association, 1958), pp. 78-79.

[13] John Henry Newman sums up the matter with his usual eloquence, "Justification is an announcement or fiat of Almighty God, which breaks upon the gloom of our natural state as the Creative Word upon Chaos; that it declares the soul righteous, and in that declaration, on the one hand, conveys pardon for its past sins, and on the other makes it actually righteous." *Lectures on the Doctrine of Justification* (London, Oxford, and Cambridge: Rivingtons, 1874), p. 83.

[14] "Hence divine sonship formally consists in an impression of the hypostatic likeness of the Only-begotten Son of God…" Joseph Pohle, *Grace: Actual and Habitual* (St. Louis: B. Herder Book Co., 1929), p. 360.

[15] Robert W. Gleason S.J. states, "The two, infusion of grace and remission of sin, are simultaneous in the order of time, but in the order of casual prior-

ity the infusion of grace is prior, since it brings about the remission of sin."
Grace (New York: Sheed & Ward, Inc., 1962), p. 97.

[16] Scheeben explains, "To join together again the severed strands of the
supernatural bond with God, no mere change of the direction of man's will
can suffice. If man is to be reunited to God as Father, God himself must
raise him up again to His side, and through the Holy Spirit must pour forth
into man's heart filial love for Himself. If the sinner is to be freed from
God's disfavor, it will not at all suffice for God to cover up the sinful deed
with the cloak of forgetfulness, and simply remit the guilt in response to
the sinner's repentance. To forgive the sin fully, God must again confer on
man that favor and grace which He had bestowed on him before he sinned.
God must again draw man up to His bosom as His child, regenerate him to
new divine life, and again clothe him with the garment of His children, the
splendor of His own nature and glory." *The Mysteries of Christianity*, pp.
615-616.

[17] Scheeben elaborates, "That is to say, as long as we think of ourselves
merely as God's creatures and bondsmen, we can be objects of the divine
wrath and abhorrence on account of the guilt we have loaded upon ourselves... God is ever entitled to adequate satisfaction, which the creature
himself can never render. But if...we pass from the condition of bondage to
the bosom of God by a supernatural birth, that is, if we become God's children, we immediately cease to be objects of God's wrath and abhorrence."
Ibid., p. 619.

[18] The legal satisfactory aspect of the atonement is not denied by Catholics.
Scheeben, for example, recognizes the "infinite value of Christ's satisfac-
tions, by which the debt is literally paid and cancelled." Ibid., p. 617. What
is primary, however, is the paternal act of the father with regard to the child,
not the juridical act of the judge, with regard to the criminal. Now the child
has been a criminal, so Christ dies to take the punishment and in his suffering, he does have that vicarious role.

[19] "It is called actual because it is not permanent or inherent, but a transient
divine influence upon the soul." W. Wilmers, S.J. *Handbook of the Christian
Religion* (New York: Benziger Brothers, 1921), p. 282.

[20] Ibid.

[21] Ibid.

[22] While sanctifying grace removes sin from the soul in baptism, the inclina-
tion towards sin, or concupiscence, remains in the justified person. Now a

person can commit venial sin and remain in a state of grace, but he loses this grace by committing mortal sin. As Trent states, "…it must be maintained that the grace of justification once received is lost not only by infidelity… but also by every other mortal sin." (Sess. VI, Chap. XV) See Peter Fransen, S.J. *The New Life of Grace* (London: Geoffrey Chapman, 1969), pp. 250-272.

[23] As Cardinal Newman states, "….He justifies us, not only in word, but in power, bringing the ark with its mercy seat into the temple of our hearts; manifesting, setting up there His new kingdom and the power and glory of His Cross." *Lectures on Justification*, pp. 102-103.

[24] In defense of this idea, some Catholics point to the justification of Abraham cited in Romans 4:3: "For what does the Scripture say? And Abraham believed God, and it was reckoned to him as righteousness." In this passage, Paul quotes from Genesis 15:6 in order to show that Abraham was justified by faith and not circumcision (in order to refute the Judaizers), for he was not circumcised until Genesis 17. The Catholics maintain that Paul also refutes the evangelical interpretation, for it is apparent that "Abraham was," as Myles M. Bourke points out, "put into a condition of friendship with God (cf. Is. 41:8) by his first response to the call and promise of God narrated in Genesis 12:1" "St. Paul and the Justification of Abraham," *Bible Today* 10 (Feb. 1964) p. 649. Abraham was justified in Genesis 12, before he was declared righteous in Genesis 15. This declaration, therefore, could not, as evangelicals believe, refer to Abraham's conversion; in this passage then, justification is a process.

[25] It is beyond the scope of this essay to discuss the Catholic sacramental system in any detail. For a good introduction, see Colman E. O'Neil, O.P. *Meeting Christ in the Sacraments* (Staten Island, New York: Alba House, 1964).

[26] While this grace is conveyed *ex opere operato*, the sacraments are of no positive value without real faith. Louis Bouyer, the distinguished French Oratorian, explains, "The guiding principle of Catholic ascetical teaching has always been the necessity of a personal effort from each individual – from which no person or thing can absolve him—to appropriate the spiritual riches of faith and the sacraments…neither adherence to the faith of the Church, nor the sharing in its rites and sacraments, are of the least value to us apart from an effort no one can make in our stead, the effort to carry faith in our lives, to make the grace of the sacraments fecundate our lives. Without this interior response, authentic and personal, so we are assured by the whole Catholic tradition, the most scrupulous observance of the externals of

religion, the most verbally correct profession of the faith of the Church will, in effect, be quite useless to us and will serve to our own condemnation." *The Spirit and Forms of Protestantism*, pp. 112-113.

[27] Joseph Pohle explains, "Being our father by adoption, God is bound to provide us with food worthy of a divine progenitor. The food He gives us (the Holy Eucharist) corresponds to our dignity as His children, sustains us in this sublime relation, and at the same time constitutes the pledge of a glorious resurrection and an eternal beatitude." *Grace: Actual and Habitual*, p.360.

[28] Works in the Catholic sense, however, are themselves gratuitous. Gleason states, "Our justice is still gratuitous even when it depends upon our works, because the radical principle for all merit is itself the original gift of grace. While our justification implies activity on our part, still the only reason that we can act in the divine order is the original gift of grace..." *Grace*, p. 92.

[29] Obedience and faith are inseparable, and are both a result of grace. Cardinal Newman's observation clears up the matter, "It seems, then, that whereas Faith on our part fitly corresponds, or is the correlative, as it is called, to grace on God's part, Sacraments are but the manifestation of grace, and good works are but the manifestation of faith; so that whether we say we are justified by faith, or by works or by Sacraments, all these but mean this one doctrine, that we are justified by grace, which is given through Sacraments, impetrated by faith, manifested in works." Newman, *Lectures on Justification*, p. 303.

[30] For example, Matt. 10:42, 19:29, 25:35-40; II Cor.4:17, 5:10, II Tim. 4:7-8. See Cuttaz, *Our Life of Grace*, p. 239.

[31] Cuttaz states, "God's pledge to reward good works by the gift of new degrees of participation in His happiness is an effect of His love for His children. It makes them share even now in His own divine life, thus giving them the means of intensifying at will their supernatural life and dignity and their future beatitude." Ibid., p. 243.

[32] Gleason explains, "It is with no abdication of His limitless rule that He graciously binds Himself to reward our good actions. In doing so He rewards His own goodness, for the source of all merit is the gift of grace...It is only His promise to reward us that enables us to claim a reward." Grace, pp. 173-174.

[33] The family is the covenantal motif throughout Scripture, according to some theologians. The eminent Roman Catholic OT scholar D.J. McCarthy, for example, understands the covenant in terms of a family relationship. See

his *Treaty and Covenant* (Rome: Biblical Institute, 1963), p. 177.

[34] M.J. Scheeben, writing in the 19th century, makes this important appeal, "...both factors comprised in justification—the remission of sin and the assimilation to our supernatural end—are rooted in the grace of divine sonship and are based on that grace. At one and the same time the grace of sonship expels all guilt from us, and infuses into us a love for God which is the love of a child or a friend.

For this reason the Council of Trent, when propounding the true nature of justification, could confine itself to the statement that it is "a transference from the state in which man is born a son of the first Adam to a state of grace and adoption of the sons of God." In these words the Council singles out the element that imparts to Christian justification its supernatural, mysterious character. We must cling to these words and make them our point of departure, if we would appreciate the full excellence of justification. If all the theologians had done this, the notion of justification would have escaped the shallow and muddled treatment that has so often disfigured it."

Scheeben, *The Mysteries of Christianity*, pp. 622-623.

Works Consulted by Sola Gratia, Solo Christo:

Books

Boehl, Edward. *The Reformed Doctrine of Justification*. Grand Rapids, Michigan: Eerdmans, 1946.

Bouyer, Louis. *The Spirit and Forms of Protestantism*. Westminster, Maryland: The Newman Press, 1956.

Buchanan, James. *The Doctrine of Justification*. London: The Banner of Truth Trust, 1961.

Cuskelly, E.J. *God's Gracious Design: A New Look at Catholic Doctrine*. Westminster, Maryland: The Newman Press, 1965.

Cuttaz, Cannon F. *Our Life of Grace*. Chicago, Illinois: Fides Publishers Association, 1958.

Dubarle, A.M. *The Biblical Doctrine of Original Sin*. New York: Herder and Herder, 1964.

Fransen, Peter. *The New Life of Grace*. London: Geoffrey Chapman, 1969.

Garrigou-Lagrange, Reginald. *Grace*. St. Louis B. Herder Book Co., 1952.

Gleason, Robert W. *Grace*. New York: Sheed & Ward, Inc., 1962.

Jedin, Hubert. *Papal Legate at the Council of Trent: Cardinal Seripando*. St. Louis: B. Herder Book Co., 1947.

Kung, Hans. *Grace: The Doctrine of Karl Barth and a Catholic Reflection*. New York, Thomas Nelson & Sons, 1964.

Mersch, Emile. *The Theology of the Mystical Body*. St. Louis: B. Herder Book Co., 1951.

Newman, John Henry. *Lectures on the Doctrine of Justification*. London, Oxford, and Cambridge: Rivingtons, 1874.

O'Neil, Colman E. *Meeting Christ in the Sacraments*. Staten Island, New York: Alba House, 1964.

Scheeben, Matthias Joseph. *The Mysteries of Christianity*. St. Louis: B. Herder Book Co., 1946.

Schmaus, Michael. *Justification and the Last Things*. Kansas City: Sheed and Ward, 1977.

Wilmers, W. *Handbook of the Christian Religion*. New York: Benziger Brothers, 1921.

Journal Articles

Bourke, Myles M. "*St. Paul and the Justification of Abraham*." Bible today 10 (February 1964): 643-649.

Brinsmead, Robert. "*Further Observations on the Order of Justification and Regeneration.*" Present Truth 5/6 (September 1976):17.

Crowley, Patrick. "*Justification by Faith in St. Paul.*" Scripture 18/44 (October 1966):97-111.

Hill, William J. "*Justification in Catholic Theology Today.*" The Thomist 30/3 (July 1966): 205-227.

McCue, James F. "*Ecumenical Reflection on Justification.*" The Ecumenist 18/4 (May-June 1980):49-53.

Moeller, Charles. "Grace and Justification." *Lumen Vitae* 19 (1964): 219-230.

Glossary

[1] Strong's numbers refer to the numbering system in the Greek and Hebrew dictionaries found in the back section of *Strong's Exhaustive Concordance of the Bible* (by James Strong). Strong's numbers allow readers of the English Bible to find the original Hebrew and Greek words along with a brief definition.

CCC, glossary: "merit." See also nos. 2006–11.

About the Author

Steve Wood was an instructor in the Calvary Chapel Bible School following graduation from Southern California College (Assemblies of God). He has led youth, campus, and pro-life ministries. After graduating from Gordon-Conwell Theological Seminary, he served as an Evangelical pastor (PCA) and church planter before entering the Catholic Church in 1990.

Responding to a challenge from Pope John Paul II to strengthen families, he started the Family Life Center International in 1992. Over the past twenty-five years, the Family Life Center has networked with thousands of families in over 100 countries.

Steve is also the founder of St. Joseph's Covenant Keepers, a movement that seeks to transform society through the transformation of fathers and families. Pope Benedict XVI bestowed on Steve the Papal Honor: *Pro Ecclesia et Pontifice* (For Church and Pope), in recognition of his service with St. Joseph's Covenant Keepers.

Steve is also the longtime host of the Faith & Family radio broadcasts. *Grace and Justification* is his fifth book.

Made in the USA
Lexington, KY
22 September 2017